THE GRACE OF ENOUGH

"We loved this fantastic story of faith, family, and discovering the joy of living on less. This book is a spiritually inspiring reminder to pause and reflect on how we can step away from the throwaway culture."

Michele Faehnle and Emily Jaminet
Authors of *Divine Mercy for Moms*

"What sort of life is God calling you to live? That's the question Haley Stewart's delightful yet challenging new book invites you to consider. Though your answer may be different from hers, her honest sharing and insightful suggestions will invite you into a rich reflection on your own experience that will help you recognize that God is always enough."

Mary Elizabeth Sperry
Author of *Making Room for God*

"Not everyone may follow Haley Stewart's family's example of selling their house and moving to a farm, but her meditations on the subject sharpened my hunger for the goods she was chasing, some as simple as the whole family being able to share lunch."

Leah Libresco Sargeant
Author of *Arriving at Amen*

"Prophets wake us to our true state, call upon us to be better than we are, and demand that we think hard about the life we are living. And thus we shy away from prophets. Haley Stewart, however, won't let us escape so easily. Hers is a genuinely prophetic voice but one so full of fun and the sheer joy of living that she thoroughly charmed and convinced me. A wonderfully wise book for our confusing and misguided era."

Paula Huston
Author of *One Ordinary Sunday*

"The collective conscious of our culture is desperately crying out for this message. Haley Stewart shows how to practically and bravely embrace the profound simplicity of living the Gospel of Jesus Christ. Stewart's book connects with our longings for living the simple but abundant joy of Christ."

Leah Darrow
International Catholic speaker and author of *The Other Side of Beauty*

"An antidote to throwaway culture; a blueprint to living a fulfilling life."

From the foreword by **Brandon Vogt**
Content director of Word on Fire Catholic Ministries
and author of *Why I Am Catholic*

"If you've ever yearned to make radical changes to your life that will bring you lasting satisfaction, this is the book for you."

Jennifer Fulwiler
SiriusXM radio host and author of *Something Other Than God*

"Our culture has proposed that the path to freedom entails working harder in order to have more. Our faith proposes a radically different idea. In this lovely book, Haley Stewart explores the idea of living simply—and it's an idea that has the power to change the world."

Tommy Tighe
Editor of *The Catholic Hipster Handbook*

PURSUING LESS AND LIVING MORE
IN A THROWAWAY CULTURE

THE GRACE
OF ENOUGH

HALEY STEWART

AVE MARIA PRESS AVE Notre Dame, Indiana

© 2018 by Haley Stewart

Founded in 1865, Ave Maria Press is a ministry of the United States Province of Holy Cross.

www.avemariapress.com

Paperback: ISBN-13 978-1-59471-817-5

E-book: ISBN-13 978-1-59471-818-2

Cover image © iStock.com.

Cover and text design by Katherine Robinson.

Printed and bound in the United States of America.

Library of Congress Cataloging-in-Publication Data is available.

To Daniel.

All my

best adventures

have been

with you.

It is Jesus in fact that you seek when you dream of happiness; he is waiting for you when nothing else you find satisfies you; he is the beauty to which you are so attracted; it is he who provokes you with that thirst for fullness that will not let you settle for compromise; it is he who urges you to shed the masks of a false life; it is he who reads in your hearts your most genuine choices, the choices that others try to stifle. It is Jesus who stirs in you the desire to do something great with your lives, the will to follow an ideal, the refusal to allow yourselves to be grounded down by mediocrity, the courage to commit yourselves humbly and patiently to improving yourselves and society, making the world more human and more fraternal.

—St. John Paul II

CONTENTS

FOREWORD
BY BRANDON VOGT

It was probably one of the most disconcerting parts of converting to Catholicism. As a young college student unexpectedly interested in the Catholic Church, I was especially captivated by the saints. Many of these radical men and women gave up everything to serve the poor and marginalized, and they were inordinately joyful—probably the happiest people I had encountered in any biography or history book. Something about their lives screamed, "If you want to be truly happy, this is the right way to live." So I became Catholic, yearning to follow their path.

But there was dissonance. The blueprint I had received growing up indicated that the keys to happiness were not simplicity and generosity but accumulation and control. I had to get married, move to the suburbs, get a high-paying job or start a business, buy a large house, and fill it up with things. Perhaps have a child or two as I climbed to the top and swallowed as much of the world as I could hold— always more, more, more. I needed to be secure, safe, and totally independent. That was the way to the good life, or so I thought.

So I followed that path. After graduating college, I got married, moved to the suburbs, got a cushy white-collar office job, bought a house, and started accumulating—electronics, furniture, toys, clothes, a garage full of stuff. My wife and I began having children, and we settled in for what we expected would be seventy years of safe, comfy, predictable suburban bliss, the same sort of life our parents had.

Yet a set of questions haunted me: "Is this honestly fulfilling? Is this really the good life?" Those questions wouldn't stop bothering me for two reasons:

First, the saints' example still lingered in the back of my mind. I knew my consumption-based lifestyle was nothing like theirs. I wanted more and more; they wanted less and less. I chased security and independence; they leaned on God and community. My life was fast-paced and overscheduled; theirs was steady and methodical.

Second, I also knew, at my most honest moments, that while my consumption-based life had momentary delights, there was no enduring satisfaction. To use an image from St. John of the Cross, no finite goods could ever, even in principle, fill my heart's infinite caverns. Man cannot live on big screens and 401(k)s alone.

The problem was that I still didn't have an alternative. While I loved the saints and felt drawn to their way of life, I just couldn't see how to imitate their lives today. I admired Dorothy Day's radical commitment to the poor, how she welcomed beggars and homeless people, planted small gardens, and revolved her day around hospitality, charity, and simplicity. But how could a twenty-something father living in the suburbs come anywhere close to that? Most of my day was spent in a drab office tapping away on a computer—the only connection I had to creation was mowing my yard once a week and seeing the occasional squirrel. And living in the suburbs meant I rarely even encountered poor people, much less served them.

Similarly, I felt drawn to Mother Teresa. Her extraordinary commitment to the sick and dying and her vibrant community life were profoundly compelling. As I read stories about her, I realized that she clearly understood what mattered (love, prayer, selflessness, the works of mercy, community) and what didn't (wealth, pleasure, power, honor). That clarity produced a remarkable joy in her. But again, I thought, how in the world could I imitate her? She preached simplicity, but I felt tethered to my many possessions. She encouraged community, yet I didn't even know my next-door neighbors.

All of this troubled me. I didn't know the solution, but I knew, deep in my bones, that the consumption lifestyle wasn't it. Pope Francis later named the problem for me—throwaway culture—which he described as not only a culture but a mindset, a materialistic vision based on consumption, control, and valuing things over people.

I came to understand that the promised happiness of throwaway culture is a lie, though a tempting one. And I began to see that the standard blueprint I had been sold, to work harder to get more, was a dead-end road to dissatisfaction. And I knew it.

Which brings me, finally, to this excellent book. Oh, how I wish Haley Stewart had written it ten years ago! It would have saved my wife and I so much trouble and given us the practical vision we desperately craved. This book paints the solution we had such difficulty finding. My wife and I eventually sold our house, moved out to a five-acre plot of land in the country, and intentionally reset our lives. We doubled down on family, holiness, community, and creation. We now try to arrange our lives around those pillars. We have six children, eight goats, thirty chickens, and a garden. Our kids spend much of their day playing in trees, setting up "ninja courses," and creeping around the woods. We host big dinner parties, with dozens of people, to encourage community. I now work from home, which means I'm rarely apart from my wife and kids. It's a totally different life, and we love it, but it took lots of struggle and blind groping to get here. This book would have saved us much trouble.

As you'll see, Haley and her family model what it looks like for a modern family to live an intentional, radical Gospel lifestyle—like the saints who drew me to the Church. Here you'll discover a refreshing paradigm. Instead of making decisions that optimize their family's comfort, they ask, "What will bring our family closer to each other, and to God? What will generate more beauty and transcendence?

What will facilitate deeper community?" This is a radical paradigm, and it's led to some curious decisions, at least from the perspective of throwaway culture. Instead of the expedient, they prefer the meaningful. Instead of the efficient, they choose the beautiful. Instead of wanting more, they delight in less.

And none of this was by accident. They didn't just slip aimlessly into this lifestyle. It was intentional (in fact, you'll spot that word at least two dozen times.) They got clear about their family's sense of *mission*, which drove their major decisions—where to live, what jobs to take, what food to eat, what art to hang on the walls. They didn't casually make those decisions and then let their family identity take form around them. Instead, they articulated what their family is about, what is most important to them, and let their priorities and decisions flow from that.

Although Haley's family (along with mine) gave up the suburbs and moved to the country, she is careful to note that you don't have to follow that exact path: "Simplicity at my house is going to look different from simplicity at your house." Perhaps your family will flourish better in the city, suburbs, or in an apartment rather than on a farm. It's not *where* you live that's important but *how*. And that's what Haley focuses on.

This book is an antidote to throwaway culture, a blueprint to living a fulfilling life. What St. Benedict did for the early monastics, Haley has done for modern suburbanites and families: provide a compelling rule, a practical life plan, one centered on community, simplicity, and charity.

The stories are colorful and wonderful. (Do you know anyone else who *voluntarily* lived on a farm without flushing toilets? You'll never look at sawdust the same way again.) But each story illustrates deeper principles. Haley highlights the emptiness of throwaway culture but also a cure: simple practices that can shift you toward a more satisfying path.

What does it look like *today* to live as saints did in past centuries? You'll find one vision here. But don't rush through the book—read it slowly and carefully. Don't just marvel at Haley and her wonderful family and say, "That's impressive and nice for them. I'm glad they're happy, but we could never adjust our lives in that way." Instead ask yourself, "What small steps can I take to rebel against throwaway culture? What would it look like in ten, twenty, or thirty years if my family lived out of an alternate paradigm?"

Haley's book shouted something I wish I had heard ten years ago: stop chasing throwaway culture. It is a lie, and it will not make you happy. But here is another path, and it's one that will deliver what you crave: enough.

Introduction:
Throwaway Culture and Its
Revolutionary Gospel Antidote

> Human beings are themselves considered consumer
> goods to be used and then discarded. We have created
> a "throw away" culture which is now spreading.
> —Pope Francis, *Evangelii Gaudium*

The door of the moving pod came down with a clang. My
husband, Daniel, locked it and we took a step back to take in
the sight: all our worldly goods encased in the small metal
square, ready to be shipped halfway across the country. It
was midnight but still 85 degrees and muggy, as July in
Florida tends to be even after the sun goes down. Our three
kids were asleep at Grandma's house as we stood holding
hands in the dark driveway that was still technically ours
for a few more hours.

We would soon be leaving everything we knew to
move to a farm in Texas to pursue a completely different
kind of life. The finality of the pod lock clicking into place
made it all seem real. Daniel put his arm around me and
kissed the top of my head. Butterflies of fear fluttered in my
stomach, and I knew Daniel felt the same way. Although
we were ready to see what the future held, we couldn't
help but feel anxious over our impending move; it seemed
to go against all the cultural expectations of seeking security, wealth, and the house in the suburbs with the white

picket fence. Providing for and offering safety to your family is part of every parent's job, but what if the pursuit of those good things above all else causes us to lose sight of essential things such as nurturing the family itself? We were exhausted and disillusioned with the rat race and the expectation that we should pursue more, more, *more*. We were ready to say, "Enough!" Leaving a season of security was scary, but we had hope that the path ahead would be a way forward in which our family could truly thrive.

THE GOSPEL AND THROWAWAY CULTURE

Our culture presents the world as a cosmic supermarket. All of God's creation—even our relationships to other people—is there for us to consume, expendable when it becomes difficult or requires sacrifice. We're told that happiness is within our grasp if we can only buy enough, acquire enough, achieve enough. Yet in our pursuit of more, we find only a larger and larger void needing to be filled. If there is one word to describe modern culture, it might be *unsatisfied*. No matter how much we have, it's never enough.

This hunger for something more that so many of us experience is a result of the throwaway culture that Pope Francis warns against: the idea that God's earth and his creatures are commodities to be used and discarded when they become unwanted. This attitude so saturates the culture we live in that it can permeate our worldview without us even realizing we've adopted it. It creeps into everything from seemingly minor daily occurrences to grave matters. As Catholics, it might be easy to see how evils such as euthanasia or abortion stem from a throwaway culture that views even human beings as consumable, to be disposed of if inconvenient. Maybe we can see the same attitude at play when a friend describes how being on Tinder makes her feel like an object for someone else's consumption or rejection when potential hookups swipe past her. We watch governments, corporations, and individuals exhaust the resources of God's creation, ignoring the wreckage in their wake. These examples seem obvious, but what about when I decide to binge a TV show on Netflix instead of spending time with my family or answering the call to hospitality and community? What about when I purchase more than I need and throw out the leftovers as trash? Or when I consider my time to be too important to stop and get to know my neighbors? Anytime we treat those God loves as inconveniences and annoyances rather than unrepeatable, irreplaceable creatures made in the very image of God, we are acting in accordance with the throwaway culture. Anytime we fail to see and respect God's creation with the wonder it deserves, we fall short of the Gospel.

Obviously not all sins carry the same moral weight. Purchasing more than you need is not as grave a sin as euthanasia is. Yet both these things reflect a consumerist mentality, and both are symptomatic of a failure to love. The throwaway culture can never satisfy the human heart. We long for more because we were made for more.

Thankfully our lot isn't hopeless, because we have the Gospel, the antidote to the throwaway culture. It calls us to the kind of happiness that is only achievable when we are in right relationship with our God, his world, and our fellow man. Discarding this consumerist view and replacing it with the teachings of Christ will involve fighting a system of thought that is often adhered to by both political parties in America and is even pervasive in many strains of Christian culture. It's everywhere. This is why rejecting the throwaway culture can be difficult and lonely, and will undoubtedly leave you feeling politically homeless. But as the brilliant twentieth-century Southern Catholic writer Flannery O'Connor notes, "The truth does not change according to our ability to stomach it emotionally."[1] It's not an easy road, but leaving behind this culture of death opens us up to allow new life to grow.

In this book I share the story of my family's crazy experiment to leave suburban America and its temptations to affluence-focused life to pursue a family-focused life on a nonprofit, sustainable agriculture farm for one year. The seeds of discontent that took root and pushed us into this new adventure have continued to bear fruit since we transitioned back into urban life. Our experience of living with less confirmed for us that there is great joy to be found in the wisdom and tradition of the Church and that many of the virtues of simplicity and community lost in recent generations are worth rediscovering.

ARE YOU READY?

A word of caution: Those who decide to go against the grain and live out the Gospel in a way that is so countercultural are not promised success, health, or wealth. Yet the scriptures tell us that our Lord comes that we might have "life and have it more abundantly" (Jn 10:10). This fullness of life is what my family sought when we left the American dream behind. While our path to live the Gospel in the midst of throwaway culture will likely look different than yours (not everyone needs to drop everything and move to a farm), it's likely forged from the same sense of dissatisfaction with prevailing cultural values and the same longing for a better life. And that is a good place to begin.

How do you start living in this odd, revolutionary way? How do you extricate yourself from throwaway culture and live out the Gospel values in your own home and family? I believe that the key to shifting our worldview, to pursuing less and living more, is to develop virtue by taking on practices that, little by little, transform us. This kind of growth won't occur if we passively sit and wish for virtue to spring up spontaneously and effortlessly in our hearts. We can and must actively pursue virtue by taking up practices and habits that cultivate it.

Each time we trade affluence for a family-centered life, choose simplicity over excess, or practice holy hospitality, we align ourselves with the teachings of Christ and the Church. We redirect our hearts toward embracing the Christian life in ways that better orient our hearts toward God—ways that, sadly, have fallen out of fashion. While our parents' generation benefitted from living in a society in which the remnants of key virtues were still woven into the social fabric, having been handed down by our great-grandparents, the millennial generation has come of age in a disconnected world. But the situation is far from hopeless.

This disconnection we experience in modern life has brought about a deep thirst for something transcendent. Movements that reject the throwaway culture can seem like a soft whisper against the powerful crashing waves of consumerism. But this whisper is getting louder. While this longing may not lead people right into the arms of the Church as it did for my husband and me, it is, at the very least, inspiring people to view our consumerism with increased skepticism and to seek alternatives. We are seeing a resurgence of habits that can help us reorient ourselves toward the Gospel. Some of these practices are living simply, offering hospitality, reviving food culture, reconnecting with the land, nurturing community, prioritizing beauty, developing a sense of wonder, being intentional about technology, seeking authentic intimacy, and centering life around home, family, and relationships.

If you are interested in learning more about these things, keep reading—this book is a simple invitation to embrace this life of simple joy. In each chapter, I reflect on specific practices such as simplicity, hospitality, or openness to life with stories from our journey and offer ideas for implementing them in your own life. These virtues and practices are anchored in the Gospel and the wisdom of the past. By nurturing these habits, you can join all the others seeking to turn the tide of the throwaway culture.

The simple practices we'll discuss—such as owning and purchasing less, cooking and eating dinner together, and opening our homes to offer hospitality—are nothing novel, uncharted, or shocking. But in a society saturated with materialism, technology, and self-obsession, these habits and shifts in perspective might feel countercultural, even revolutionary. In many ways they are revolutionary—a Gospel revolution.

Bear in mind that I'm not a theologian, sustainability expert, or anyone's life coach. And I'm certainly not claiming to be a perfect example of the virtues on which this book reflects. I'm a work in progress, a Catholic convert and mother of four desiring the same thing you desire: to be fully alive to the truth of the Gospel and to flourish, despite being smack-dab in the middle of the throwaway culture.

I want to encourage you to consider that the quest to live the Gospel in the modern world is not only possible but also joyful (albeit difficult). We all have different circumstances: as a married couple with young kids, our path is going to look very different from that of someone who just graduated from college or is an empty nester. This book isn't a manual or a checklist that requires conformity. It's a series of reflections on how Daniel and I sought to develop a posture of intentional living as Christians and caretakers of the land and lives we've been given. My prayer is that those ideas will be applicable to anyone desiring to be anchored with these deep Gospel truths rather than being swept away in the current of consumerism and secularism. Whether you're a millennial or a baby boomer, a single person or a father of ten kids, a person discerning a call to religious life, consecrated life, or the vocation of marriage, this shift away from throwaway culture is something you can pursue. And the results will be well worth your effort.

I know this to be true because as we incorporated these practices into our own lives, as we attempted to shift our mind-set to be more consistent with the Gospel, our family began to thrive in a beautiful new way. At the end of this book is a series of questions that may help you discern for yourself—on your own or with a group of friends—how you can better put these virtues to practice in your own life.

Thank you for allowing me to share my story with you. If there is something in particular that resonated with you or that has challenged you to live your faith in a deeper way, I would love to hear from you. You can reach out to me through my blog, *Carrots for Michaelmas* (www.carrots-formichaelmas.com). God bless you!

PART I

RETURNING
TO OUR ROOTS

1

NO TURNING BACK: TRADING SECURITY FOR TOGETHERNESS

Faith is one foot on the ground, one foot in the air, and a queasy feeling in the stomach.
                                    —Mother Angelica

It felt as though a ten-pound stone was lodged in the pit of my stomach. I had lost my appetite and sleep was elusive. But there was no going back. We had made up our minds, and I had no doubts that we were making the right decision. What I agonized over was how I would *explain*.

How could I communicate to friends and family why we, twenty-something Floridians with three kids, were putting our darling starter home, with its 1940s charm, on the market? It had been our first house, the house to which we'd brought two of our babies home from the hospital, with a great fenced-in backyard where our kids played. How could we give it up so easily?

How could I explain why Daniel was leaving a stable and secure office job at a prison software company—a job that paid our bills and supported our family yet left him strangely dissatisfied? We should have been happy. So how was I going to make people understand that we wanted to pursue a different kind of life for our family, and that it entailed Daniel quitting his job to take an internship halfway across the country on a sustainable agriculture training farm that offered only a small monthly stipend?

We were embarking on a journey that would either be the adventure of a lifetime or the most foolish decision of our lives. As we stayed up late discussing plans, it was clear that this was the craziest thing we'd ever done—and we've made our fair share of countercultural decisions. We married after my sophomore year of college at the venerable age of twenty. We converted to Catholicism soon after graduating from our Baptist college. We'd had three of our babies within four years. But this move would take the cake.

We were leaving everything conventional behind and moving to a 650-square-foot apartment on a working farm with no flushing toilets in central Texas, several states away from family. Would anyone understand? Would we be able to support our three young children? Were we crazy even to think about doing this?

Some would surely think we had lost our minds. After all, we had originally moved to Florida after college to be close to our extended family after our first child was born. We knew we needed the extra support. What would happen to us if this new adventure didn't work out? What if we hated farming? What if parenting and homeschooling several states away from our extended family was too much? What if living in such close quarters with all three kids and no free babysitting compliments of grandparents turned out to be more than we could handle? What if potty training a toddler on a compost toilet pushed me to the brink of insanity?

What was so bad about our life as it was, anyway?

I braced myself for those questions and worried about others that might be verbalized about our plan. After all, there was no denying we were doing something pretty out of the ordinary. And I wasn't wrong about the response. I'll admit to getting some raised eyebrows and even the insinuation that people who can pay their bills are fools to make career changes, no matter how miserable their jobs are. It sure didn't sound very *responsible*. When I announced our plan on my blog, some of the comments were even angry: "How dare you refuse to be satisfied with conventional American life, you entitled millennial?" But I had braced myself for that.

What I wasn't expecting was the overwhelmingly positive response to our news. Over and over emails flew into my inbox from blog readers saying "I wish we could do something like this!" Friends kept admitting they were jealous of our endeavor to lead a simpler life and choose this unconventional path. We realized that we were certainly not the only ones who were discontented with what conventional American culture was offering us.

THE ROOT OF THE PROBLEM

So what was the problem with the life we were living? The truth is that we found ourselves *stuck*. In order to pay our mortgage, utilities, groceries, health insurance, and school loans, Daniel had to work long hours at a job he not only didn't love but also didn't believe in. He would leave the house by seven each morning to sit in front of a computer, testing software for prison systems—systems that don't function in the way we believe is best for society. He'd return home every night at six, just in time for dinner and bedtime, almost completely missing our children's waking hours. It wasn't what we'd envisioned for our family.

Like most families, we wanted to be able to provide for our children and raise them together. Daniel was working more than fifty hours a week, and I was working part-time while homeschooling and raising three young children in order to barely cover our bills with very frugal living: a small starter home, one vehicle, no cable, cooking at home, only necessary purchases, and buying secondhand. We wondered if working more hours could help us get ahead. At first it made sense. If Daniel worked weekends, he would bring in a bigger paycheck. But it wasn't that simple.

It turns out that working so many hours is actually an *expensive* way to live. Working more hours meant we had less time, so we ended up spending money on services we could otherwise handle ourselves. We quickly blew through our monthly food budget. Instead of spending our time cooking together as a family on a consistent basis, we had no time to meal plan and cook at home. We found ourselves eating out or picking up takeout more often. These extra expenses erased the hard work spent trying to stay afloat, and we had gained neither quality of life nor more family time.

Increasing work hours also results in additional hidden costs in daycare, car payments, fuel, and other expenses that emerge when time is in such short supply. Wrapped up in this endless work cycle, we were working more and seeing each other less, and the increased spending made the increase to our income negligible. Working those extra hours wasn't helping us.

Especially in a post-recession economy, many people aren't working to get ahead—they're just trying to eke out a living for themselves and their families. Maybe you're already living very simply for financial stewardship reasons. Maybe you just feel stuck in the rat race and are exhausted and unsatisfied. There's certainly a catch-22 in the American pursuit of affluence. We work more so we can achieve the dream of having a nice house to enjoy. But working more means we have less time to be at our home enjoying it. We want to provide our children with prosperity but end up depriving them of what they actually need and desire—time with us.

Many of my blog readers expressed this frustration over email. They explained that they had done everything right: gone to the right schools, worked hard, completed the right internships. And they were now working jobs that weren't fulfilling, spending too much time away from their families and often still barely scraping by. They felt trapped and dissatisfied. Maybe you can relate.

We were stuck and looking for a way out. I hated knowing that Daniel was leaving home each day to count down the hours at the office, only to return to us wiped out before the rush of dinner, bath, and bedtime. He looked into other job opportunities, but between a post-recession job market and the high cost of living in Florida, we couldn't figure out how to make it work.

THE PRAYER OF SURRENDER

After months of frustration, instead of continuing to pray for a new job opportunity Daniel started praying for surrender. He pursued contentment and joy in the life we already had, despite its imperfections. He focused on the things he could do to pursue his passion for farming in the here and now: growing veggies in our front yard and caring for our flock of backyard chickens. He read books about farming and homesteading and soaked up all the knowledge he could. We tried to put down some roots and get more involved in our parish. Despite—or perhaps *because* of—his many tattoos, our parish priest asked Daniel to volunteer with the high school youth, and he began regularly serving in that ministry. We began building friendships and tried to be content in our life in Florida.

It was when we stopped trying to force changes in our lives that opportunities started to pop up that made a real change possible. Daniel was offered a paid position in youth ministry at our parish and some of my writing projects started to become more lucrative. After living paycheck to paycheck for our entire married life, we were able to save

a little bit. Maybe this was it—our chance to get unstuck!
We still didn't know exactly where we were headed, but we
kept our eyes open for the next step.

Then, in 2014, we visited Waco, Texas, where we had
gone to college, for a dear friend's wedding. On the long
drive back to Florida, all three kids miraculously fell asleep
in the van. In the unusual quiet, we started to dream a little
bit. I asked Daniel, "What would you want to do if you
could do anything—anything at all? What do you think a
good life would look like?"

"I'd want to eat three meals a day together as a family. I'd want to spend more time with the kids. And I'd
want to do good, honest work that I loved—something like
farming."

We both sighed. We knew we were nowhere close to
having the resources to purchase land, and we couldn't
imagine getting to that point on our current salaries. Then
there was the challenge of gaining the knowledge we'd
need when we were already maxed out with work. It was
a dream that seemed very far away.

Then I had an epiphany. "What about the farm where
we used to volunteer in college? The internship at the World
Hunger Relief Farm? What if we moved back to Texas, you
learned to farm, and we spent a year living and working
together—our whole family?"

We decided to pray about it. Moving our whole life
across the country for at least a year, not knowing what
would happen when the internship was over, was a tall
order. But after thinking and praying about it, we decided
to apply and see what happened. It was scary to think of
doing something so . . . well, crazy. What if we got there
and didn't like it? What if it was a disaster? But since we
already knew we were unhappy in our current situation
and staying put wouldn't solve anything, it was a risk we
were willing to take.

THE PRICE OF A DREAM

Giving our family the opportunity to live on a working farm had many draws: space for our kids to explore and roam, educational opportunities for homeschooling aplenty, eating three meals a day together as a family, doing work that we could be proud of at the end of the day, and developing valuable skills. But our decision to apply for the internship wasn't exclusively about a desire to farm. The life we were living was getting us nowhere we wanted to go, and we wanted to remove ourselves from the cyclical model of affluence that stems from the grasping, greedy lies of throwaway culture.

What we truly desired was more time together as a family and work that made us come alive. Maybe the answer to our problems was not more—more money, more hours, more stuff. Maybe the answer was asking for the grace to be contented with *enough* and a willingness to make do with *less*—even if that included no flushing toilets. While it may have sounded a little crazy, our decision to live on the farm for a year made perfect sense.

But quitting jobs in Florida and relocating far away from family was much easier said than done. There were many challenges ahead, not least of which was preparing to put our house on the market for this potential move. We wouldn't hear back about the internship program for a few months, but we couldn't wait that long to start trying to sell our house. We didn't have the financial buffer to be paying our mortgage once Daniel quit his job. Our house needed to sell *before* we left Florida. We took a leap of faith that he would get the internship and called a realtor to talk about what we needed to do to get the ball rolling on the sale. We spent a couple of weeks getting the house show-ready, then took a deep breath and listed it.

There we were with a house on the market and a hope that Daniel's internship application would be accepted. Would the house sell in time? Would the internship come through, or would we sell our home only to discover that we had nowhere to go? Life felt like one big question mark, and I don't deal with question marks very well.

One morning I was racing around the house, trying to go through boxes of the kids' clothes and decide what to pack and what to donate, helping the six-year-old with his math problems, and making snacks for the toddlers. I realized my heart was racing, and I felt as if I couldn't breathe. I walked to my room and sat down on my bed while the kids played in the living room. I struggled to get air into my lungs. *This must be what a panic attack feels like,* I said to myself. The unknowns were getting to me. My fears and anxieties felt as if they were choking me. *Lord, please don't let this whole thing be a big mistake,* I prayed.

As much as I tried not to worry, I kept imagining a nightmare of everything falling apart and having to explain, "Well, actually we had a lovely little house and could pay our bills until we went crazy and tried to move across the country to a farm with no flushing toilets and now we're just wandering nomads with no idea where to go." In my imaginary scenario of doom, we were homeless, sitting by the side of the road under a hot desert sun, having just run out of water, our children cursing the sky for the misfortune of having such irresponsible idiots as parents. Were we insane? I tried to keep focusing on breathing. I needed to take care of three small children. I needed to not be having a panic attack. I needed to do a thousand things to prepare for this crazy move. My breathing eventually calmed, and my heart stopped racing, but that wasn't the last panic attack I'd have during those stressful months.

I didn't want to change my mind and give up on the plan. I didn't want things to stay as they were. And I really did believe we were moving in the right direction. But not knowing how it would all work out was killing me. I like knowing what each step ahead will look like. I like to be in control. If there's nothing productive I can do, then I still feel compelled to do *something* (even if that something is just worrying until I induce a panic attack). Admittedly it's not a very helpful attitude. Daniel, on the other hand, has the obnoxiously reasonable perspective that worrying doesn't actually improve any situation. "But aren't you scared we'll be homeless nomads?" I would pester, only to hear him chuckle, "God's always taken care of us. I don't see why he would suddenly stop now."

In addition to the anxiety, the practical aspect of selling the house while homeschooling small children in it was misery. I remember one particularly trying morning of schooling and wrangling my three kids (ages six, three, and one at the time) in the backyard. I had banished them from the house because keeping a home show-ready with small children inside it is an exercise in insanity. No sooner would I finish cleaning the kitchen than I'd turn to find my three-year-old joyfully wiping peanut butter all over the oven while the baby eagerly emptied all of the dresser drawers and laundry hampers, happily scattering their contents around each room.

Our house had been on the market for eleven weeks—eleven weeks I never want to relive. While I'm typically good at mentally moving on to "the next thing," it wasn't easy for me to emotionally detach from our first home. It was the house to which I brought two babies home from the hospital. It was the house where we really found our groove as a family. I told Daniel many times while nursing a baby on the couch as he prepped dinner, "I will never be able to love a house like I love this house." But my sentimentality was about to be tested.

We'd gotten word that Daniel had been accepted into the livestock internship at the World Hunger Relief Farm in Waco, Texas. At least we knew that if we sold our house, we would have somewhere to go (progress!). But we were down to the wire. We needed it to sell, and quickly, or we wouldn't be able to move to the farm. While we waited for someone to make us a good offer on our home, we sold, donated, or gave away more than half of our stuff. We had only lived in our house five years, but the amount of worldly goods we had acquired was dizzying. We needed to pare down our possessions until everything we owned in the world could fit in one seven-by-seven-foot moving pod to grace our tiny two-bedroom apartment at the farm. (I'll be sharing more about that process in the next chapter.) As the piles of items diminished, and the time drew closer for us to leave for Texas, my anxiety grew. I was trying to face the fact that I was not in control. I couldn't make our house sell by sheer force of will. As we inched closer to our departure date, even unflappable Daniel started to feel on edge.

We decided to call in reinforcements: *St. Joseph, care for us as you did for the Holy Family. Guide us and help us to sell our house.* Getting to know St. Joseph during this tumultuous season was a blessing that would continue to offer grace beyond the sale of our house. I had never had a devotion to Jesus' foster father until that season, but my desperation for a good buyer led me straight into his arms. The knowledge that this holy saint was interceding for us brought peace to my frenzied heart. I could imagine St. Joseph quietly working for our good as he did for Jesus and Mary. I love how St. Joseph never seems to want the spotlight. If he had joined the theater instead of becoming a carpenter, I imagine he'd be the stage manager, carefully orchestrating everything in the wings and never going onstage. It seemed like a no-brainer to put my family's needs in the hands of the patron of the family and the universal Church. Considering the way he protected the Holy Family, St. Joseph seems to be able to handle a lot of responsibility. Surely he could sort out one house sale.

It was 1:00 p.m., the sacred hour of naptime. There had been weeping and gnashing of teeth (mostly from me), but I, Haley Stewart, stressed and exhausted homeschooling mum, emerged victorious from the kids' bedrooms. All three were asleep, and I was wiped out and ready to lie on the couch doing exactly nothing apart from grasping my final thread of sanity during an hour and a half of complete silence.

Then my phone dinged with a text from the realtor. "Can I bring a potential buyer over in twenty minutes?" "Absolutely!" I replied with a smiley face emoji representing the exact opposite of my current emotional state. I crabbily threw snacks in my purse, hid some laundry in the dryer, and woke up sleeping children in order to scurry out of the house for an hour of what I expected to be complete misery with two overtired toddlers and a grumpy six-year-old. I wasn't wrong. But it turned out that waking up the kids was worth it.

Two days later I was eighty miles away, sitting on the porch of a beach house where one of my best friends was getting married. The kids had been invited too, and we had originally planned to all drive down the day of the wedding. But my wise husband practically pushed me into the maid of honor's car and sent me off to de-stress at the beach and attend all the wedding party events I had previously declined. Apparently staying home to care for the kids solo was more appealing than dealing with an imminent emotional meltdown from his stressed-out wife. Whatever the reason, bless him.

As I sat in the sun trying to get used to the sensation of not running around like a chicken with its head cut off, all my anxieties were still racing through my head. I took a deep breath and tried to drown my fears in the sunshine and one of Dorothy Sayers' mystery novels. My mantra is, if in doubt, try murder-mystery therapy. My phone rang. It was Daniel.

"We got an offer from the showing this week! The timeline is perfect; the price isn't amazing but we can live with it." I did a little dance in the sand. It was happening.

We were really doing this. We were trying out this grand experiment.

Finding the Grace of Enough: Tips for Getting Back to Basics

Choosing an unconventional path and intentionally shifting your priorities away from the throwaway culture requires thoughtful planning, a lot of work, and a willingness to sacrifice comfort. It doesn't have to be done by getting rid of half of your possessions and moving to a farm, of course. But it won't be easy.

Take stock of your life. Is it the life God wants you to be living? Are you feeling stuck? Most of us are so entrenched in the culture that it's hard to even think outside the affluence-focused box. Give yourself time to reflect and brainstorm about how you could do things differently, even if it would require taking an unusual path.

To discern our big decision to move to the farm, Daniel and I allowed ourselves a lot of space to dream about how we would like to see our family thrive and what principles we wanted to live out for our children. Even before doors opened for us to make a big shift in our work lives, we were able to begin drawing from those ideals in small but significant ways.

Leave room for flexibility and change. While our move to the farm was a great choice for our family, it wouldn't be a good fit for everyone. We know more than one family that has tried farming, for instance, and discovered that their passions lie elsewhere. By taking the opportunity to volunteer or try out a short-term arrangement, you can learn a lot about whether a step is right for your family.

Consider what changes you want to make in your life. Are those changes possible right now? Are they long-term goals you will have to slowly and patiently work toward? Try to find small ways you can make a difference today.

2

SIMPLICITY, THE PATH TO AUTHENTIC FREEDOM

> The bread you are holding back is for the hungry, the clothes you keep put away are for the naked, the shoes that are rotting away with disuse are for those who have none, the silver you keep buried in the earth is for the needy.
> —St. Basil the Great, *On Social Justice*

Paring down our possessions before our move was quite an undertaking. As we faced the colossal task, Daniel and I reminisced about August 2006 when we moved into our first apartment. It was the summer we were married, just before my junior year of college.

We fit everything we owned into our green Camry and bought an air bed from Target because we couldn't afford a mattress and bed frame. Daniel nailed together planks of wood and propped them up on flower pots to create a dining room table, and we used throw pillows for seating. Our silverware, plates, cups, bowls, and cloth napkins were wedding gifts, along with a pot and a pan, knives, and a pitcher. We splurged on a shower curtain and some towels. Daniel found an old ladder and turned it into a shelf for odds and ends. Apart from our books and clothes, that about sums up all our worldly possessions. But we didn't feel deprived; we were poor and young and in love.

In the musical *Fiddler on the Roof*, Tevya, the paterfa-milias of a large Jewish family, describes his newlywed daughter, Tzeitel, and her husband, the poor tailor Motel, by saying, "They're so happy, they don't know how miser-able they are!" That was us: too happy to notice that it was weird not to own chairs. After a couple of months, our air mattress started to leak in the wee small hours. Apparently they're not meant to be slept on *every* single night. Who knew? But we didn't feel deflated. (See what I did there?) Quite the opposite.

But *this* season of preparation for our move to the farm was a little different from newlywed life. Nine years of mar-riage (and three kids) had brought significantly more pos-sessions into our lives. We had chairs now and not just one but *four* real mattresses. Toys, books, furniture, bikes, and, as we discovered while packing, far more belongings than would fit into our farm apartment, all 650 square feet of it.

We certainly weren't alone in our acquisition of more things than we could ever use. To give just one example, a group of social scientists at the University of California, Los Angeles, recently published a study revealing that three out of four garages in the United States are too full to hold cars.[1] Simply *managing* the great volume of possessions in Amer-ican homes is a huge source of stress for families. Maintain-ing all the stuff eats into our time to such a degree that we can't even enjoy what we own. If this struggle describes you as well, you may have bought into the false freedom that more means safety, security, that you won't have to go without. Our stuff owns *us*. We pass the burden on to our children as well. While they make up only 3 percent of the world's children, American kids own 40 percent of the world's toys.[2]

This consumerist mind-set is a symptom of a deeper disease of our dissatisfaction and spiritual poverty. Pope Francis reminds us in his papal encyclical *Laudato Si'*, "When people become self-centered and self-enclosed, their greed increases. The emptier a person's heart is, the more he or she needs things to buy, own and consume" (*LS* 204).

We can never achieve true happiness with material goods—no matter what we purchase—because we were made for so much more than acquiring stuff. In *The Weight of Glory*, C. S. Lewis claims that "we are far too easily pleased."[3] We distract ourselves with what is not eternal in the way a child is too busy making mud pies to embark on "a holiday at the sea." Instead of bringing us happiness, our material goods can serve to distract us from what is truly valuable, preventing us from achieving the happiness we desire in our heart of hearts.

The idea that we'd be happier if only we had X is always a lie (unless the X is God). Yet no matter how many times I am confronted by this truth, I still fall into the trap of materialism. A couple of years ago, when our budget was tight, I noticed that some laptop/camera bags I'd had my eye on for years were on sale. I *had* to have one. I *needed* one of those bags. I'd been wanting one for years and surely, *surely* ordering one would make me happy! I would transform from the woman who carries her laptop in her purse to the woman who carries her laptop in a *fancy laptop bag*.

Over dinner I told Daniel about the sale and made what I thought to be a reasonably persuasive argument. "I don't ever buy jewelry!" I pleaded. "I don't overspend on clothes or shoes! I don't get pedicures! I deserve this bag!" Daniel's calm eyes told me everything I needed to know. He accepted my frenzied desire for this precious bag. He assured me that if I really needed this bag, we could figure out a way to make it work in our budget.

I was elated. I clicked "checkout" on that bag with joy in my heart. I kept refreshing the online tracking to see where it was on its journey to my doorstep. It finally arrived and it was . . . fine. After all that, I didn't look as cool and professional as I had imagined I would when carrying it over my shoulder. It was a little bulkier than I had antici-pated and looked far too big for my five-foot-two frame to carry around comfortably. And I woke up the next morning feeling just the same as the day before. The bag had failed to deliver on its promise. It didn't change my life.

These days it mostly takes up room in my closet and only gets pulled out for the rare occasions that I travel via airplane. It didn't fill the void. I was still me. Normal ol' me. Nothing available for purchase can satisfy what we truly desire. We can understand the truth of this but that doesn't mean it's easy to rid ourselves of the consumerist attitude that permeates our culture.

The forced simplicity of our necessary pre-farm purg-ing was good practice for us. As we took inventory of all the things we'd acquired during our marriage, we knew we needed to ruthlessly pare down our possessions in order to seek something more valuable. While Daniel was at work, I went room by room choosing things to pack, give away, sell, or trash. Sleeping bags? Keep. Lemon juicer we've used exactly never? Out you go. There was so much stuff: stuff we weren't using, stuff we'd never used, and stuff we hadn't even unpacked since our move five years prior. I was determined that nothing would come with us that wasn't absolutely necessary.

After a garage sale, many trips to Goodwill, and more filled-to-the-brim trash bags than I would ever have guessed would be necessary, more than half of our posses-sions were gone. They were all completely unnecessary items. We missed none of them. Until it was all out of the house, I didn't realize how much easier it was to keep house when extra stuff wasn't everywhere. The surfaces were clean, the closets weren't overflowing, and the carport was empty. I felt as if I could breathe. Those items weren't just taking up physical space; they had been taking up mental space. Their absence was freeing.

Even the kids noticed how pleasant it was not to live in clutter. We sent them to Grandma's house before sorting out items for our garage sale to avoid inevitable meltdowns. Something about the prospect of getting rid of a neglected item suddenly makes it an absolute favorite toy that cannot under any circumstances be parted with. (That plush tiger in the back of the closet that hasn't surfaced in years? If you're considering parting with it, Tiger will suddenly become the most important and beloved toy of all time. Trust me.) I wasn't sure my nerves could handle that kind of emotional explosion, so we made those decisions about what items were most essential and beloved when the kids were out of the house.

Our attempt was successful. While it took them months to notice that the never-played-with-but-always-scattered-across-the-floor Mega Bloks were gone, they immediately commented how delightful it was to play in a room that was no longer swimming with toys. "Thanks for cleaning our room!" they cheered. Their toy shelf was organized, and they spent more time playing instead of wallowing in an avalanche of items they rarely interacted with. After all that effort, walking around the seven-by-seven-foot moving pod that held everything we owned in the world was strange but satisfying. "It all *fits!*" we marveled.

GOODBYE, HOUSE

After all the work it took to pack and prepare the house, Daniel and I were ready to shake the dust from our feet. But the kids needed time for a real goodbye, and so before we signed papers at the closing, we walked through the house together, saying farewell to the only house they could remember living in. We let the kids wander through each room. The girls twirled around for a couple of minutes, commenting on how the lack of furniture made room for dancing.

Meanwhile, six-year-old Benjamin sobbed. The idea of moving to a farm had excited all the kids at first. Then Benjamin started to change his tune as he considered what a move would mean. "But how will I have sleepovers at Grandma's house if we live in Texas?" "Will the new owners promise to sell us back our house if we want to live here again?" "Why can't I just live in Florida and *you guys* just go to Texas?"

Poor Benjamin. He loves his routines, and he always mourns over the slightest change. Whether his day with Grandma is switched from Tuesday to Thursday or he realizes that he's outgrown a favorite sweater—it's a tragedy that only a sentimental six-year-old can comprehend. Consequently, saying goodbye to his house went about as you'd expect. Pleading, threats, tears. Getting him out the door and into the van to make it to the lawyer's office to sign closing papers on time wasn't easy. *Are we doing the right thing?* I wondered. *Is this move best for all of us, or are we setting him up for unhappiness?*

With toddlers squirming on our laps—the real estate office wasn't designed with children in mind—we initialed what felt like a thousand sheets of paper and left the room feeling lighter than air. *We don't own a house anymore and our stuff fits in a small cube!* A few days later we hit the road. Destination: Texas.

With our minivan full to bursting with boxes and the remnants of snacks we'd thrown toward the backseat to keep the kids happy and quiet on the long and exhausting drive, we turned onto the country road leading to our new home—a familiar spot to Daniel and me since we volunteered at the farm in college. We passed a little gravel parking lot and stopped next to the apartment we knew we'd be calling home for the next twelve months.

Except for the one-bedroom apartment we had rented as newlyweds, this 650-square-foot space was the smallest we'd ever inhabited. But it was bright and semiclean. It contained two tiny bedrooms—one for us and one for the three kids—plus a skinny living room, a kitchen with space for a dining table, a little hallway that led to a closet-sized laundry room, and a bathroom complete with a shower, sink—and compost toilet.

Having spent a good deal of time at the farm in the past, I wasn't surprised by the lack of flushing toilets. Simplicity was what we were seeking, and simplicity is definitely what we got. World Hunger Relief is a no-flush farm. To conserve water, the whole farm uses composting toilets that are emptied into a compost heap for fertilizing some of the pastures. Even though technically any bacteria is killed by the heat of the composting process, the "humanure" isn't used in the garden. (I can understand why. There's certainly an "ick" factor there.) Daniel volunteered to take on the task of emptying our apartment's compost toilet (which was really just a five-gallon bucket inside a frame). At least I think he volunteered. Maybe I just never offered and he took the hint, saintly man that he is.

"Okay, kids. Here's how it works," Daniel explained. "You sit on the seat like it's a regular potty and do your business. Put the toilet paper in the potty and then scoop up a cupful of sawdust from this bucket here. Dump the sawdust on top and it keeps the bathroom from getting smelly. Got it?" Our six-year-old son thought this sounded fantastic. Our three-year-old daughter did not. She swore to never, *ever* use a composting toilet. (She changed her mind a couple hours later when the situation got dire.)

The imminent task of potty training my two-year-old daughter on a composting toilet wasn't something I was looking forward to. The extra step of adding sawdust was going to be brutal when said sawdust was being poured by someone who spilled everything she carried. My predictions were right. Even with sweeping the bathroom floor multiple times a day, feeling sawdust under our feet and tracking it all over the house just became our new normal.

We unpacked our moving pod a couple days after arriving at the farm. We said hello to our bedsheets and our favorite coffee mugs. When the pod was empty, we were relieved that we hadn't crammed anything else inside it. Nothing more could have fit in our apartment. We had only the barest bones, yet we had everything we needed. It was confirmation that even a family of five doesn't need much.

Now I won't claim it was all sunshine and rainbows, living with that many people in so small a space. Bedtime with a six-year-old, a three-year-old, and a barely two-year-old all in the same bedroom is no walk in the park. With three beds in their tiny room, there was hardly any room to store stuffed animals, clothes, or toys. But they did some serious sibling bonding, and the truth is that life goes on about the same whether you live in six hundred or twelve hundred square feet of space. Cleaning the apartment took almost no time at all, and the cramped space inside pushed us to explore the world outdoors. Not once did I think, "I wish our space was bigger so we could get more stuff." Having less was a relief, like exhaling.

CHOOSE FREEDOM

When we force ourselves to live with less, we soon realize how trapped we were by having too much stuff—and how liberating it can be to get rid of it. Pope Francis warns that our culture has a very mixed-up idea of what freedom is, that the throwaway culture "leads people to believe that they are free as long as they have the supposed freedom to consume" (LS 203). We associate freedom with the expectation that the T-shirt we want will be available in every color imaginable at a dirt-cheap price. We expect hundreds of flavors of ice cream to be waiting for us at the grocery store.

Freedom is having many options to choose from, right? No. That isn't the Christian understanding of freedom at all. St. Augustine defines true freedom as the freedom to choose *the good*, not just one of many options. We are truly free when we have the power to choose not anything under the sun but what is right and good for us and for others.

Consumerism can prevent us from choosing the good by distracting us from what truly matters. Pope Francis tells us, "A constant flood of new consumer goods can baffle the heart and prevent us from cherishing each thing and each moment" (*LS* 222). He goes on to say that a return to simplicity "allows us to stop and appreciate the small things, to be grateful for the opportunities which life affords us, to be spiritually detached from what we possess, and not to succumb to sadness for what we lack" (*LS* 222). Advertising tells us every day that if we purchase more things, we'll be happier. Yet Daniel and I soon found that just the opposite is true, as Pope Francis suggests. When we live more simply, we can actually cultivate gratefulness more effectively and be less controlled by our possessions.

MORALITY AND MINIMALISM

Our culture's obsessive consumerism has become so out of control that it's only natural for us to desire something more satisfying. People are rediscovering minimalism, the idea that less is better. This can be seen in the popularity of tiny houses, capsule wardrobes, and the increasingly trendy KonMari Method of decluttering and organizing. While it became normal in recent decades to fill storage units with all the extra possessions that didn't fit in even large modern homes, the pendulum is swinging back in the other direction. As baby boomers begin to downsize, they are finding it difficult to unload a lifetime of collections, furniture, and possessions; younger generations aren't interested in becoming caretakers of it all. (This trend can take a toll on these relationships, which is another example of how our possessions can affect our well-being.)

Our excessive spending habits and tendency to hoard also have moral implications. Luke 3:11 reminds us that, "Whoever has two tunics should share with the person who has none. And whoever has food should do likewise." By spending when it is unnecessary, I am actually depriving others who do not have enough. That's a tough word, especially when I look at my closet and see dozens of unnecessary outfits. Our cultural individualism is strong on the word *mine*, but is that attitude toward our possessions truly consistent with the Gospel?

It's easy to forget that our material resources are not meant for us alone; God blesses us so that we can in turn bless others. St. Basil the Great writes, "Who are the greedy? Those who are not satisfied with what suffices for their own needs. Who are the robbers? Those who take for themselves what rightfully belongs to everyone. And you, are you not greedy? Are you not a robber? The things you received in trust as a stewardship, have you not appropriated them for yourself?"[4]

If we have more than we need, the extra doesn't belong to us. Pope Benedict XVI reminds us, "It is good for people to realize that purchasing is always a moral—and not simply economic—act. Hence *the consumer has a specific social responsibility*" (*Caritas in Veritate*, 66). What practices are we supporting when we purchase? How does the way we spend our money and consume affect not only us but others, particularly the poor?

BREAKING FREE OF STUFF

If the way we spend our money has a moral dimension, we can know that a consumerist lifestyle is not morally neutral. Yet making a change when we are so saturated in throwaway culture isn't easy. So how do we make the huge shift away from consumerism? How do we free ourselves of the stuff that has enslaved us, especially if we're not twenty-year-old newlyweds and we've slowly realized we have a stuffed garage?

God isn't calling everyone to live without a flushing toilet or to sell everything and move into a tiny apartment. Now that our year on the farm is up, we don't feel guilty about having a flushing toilet in our house. (Although after living without it for a year, a real toilet seems downright *luxurious!*)

In her wisdom, the Church doesn't give us a certain square footage limit for our homes or a number for our bank accounts. That's not how it works. There are too many factors to consider, and those tough questions are left up to lay people to discern how to be good stewards with a rightly ordered attitude to their possessions in their own families.

There are no easy, black-and-white answers to the question of how families should practice simplicity. The Vatican doesn't offer a checklist. Whenever we compare our situation to that of others, there will always be someone with more and someone with less. Our relationship to our possessions is primarily a matter of the heart, and merely acquiescing to a mantra of trendy simplicity doesn't mean we've conquered throwaway culture's siren song. While it's easy to see consumerism at play in a McMansion, someone in the tiny house movement can be just as obsessed with possessions.

Being so used to an economic system that is built upon ever-increasing consumption, it's difficult even to imagine what it was like for past generations that had neither the pressure nor the option to participate in the constant acquisition of stuff. Rather than a cycle of purchasing, consuming, and discarding, the emphasis was on preserving and maintaining the items one already had. Today this careful maintenance is almost impossible because we are constantly overwhelmed, drowning in our possessions.

It's also important to remember that, for most of us, breaking free from a consumerist mind-set doesn't happen overnight. It can be a tough and complicated process that requires careful and continual discernment. While having less certainly does help avoid the stress of being surrounded by clutter, embracing minimalism doesn't necessarily mean that we avoid having stuff-centered lives. Resisting consumerism involves more than merely buying less and having less; it also means not holding tightly to what we own—something that doesn't come easily. Yet that doesn't mean we should just throw our hands in the air and stop trying. There is hope.

A PATH TO AUTHENTIC FREEDOM

When reading Pope Francis's encyclical *Laudato Si'* (*On Care for Our Common Home*), I was inspired by the hopefulness that Christian faith brings to problems that could easily lead us to despair. The Holy Father encourages us that "human beings, while capable of the worst, are also capable of rising above themselves, choosing again what is good, and making a new start, despite their mental and social conditioning. We are able to take an honest look at ourselves, to acknowledge our deep dissatisfaction, and to embark on new paths to authentic freedom" (*LS* 205).

While the false freedom of consumerism can never make us free, we do have a chance at *authentic* freedom. We don't have to live lives of dissatisfaction and emptiness. Knowing that consumerism can never fulfill us, we have a chance and a capacity to seek something else.

Of course, simplicity at my house is going to look different from simplicity at your house. For example, we have very few toys, electronics, and extras, but we have shelves and shelves of books. I want to keep books I love. I want to share them with other people. I want my kids to read them when they get older. Living simply doesn't mean we cannot own anything. But if our possessions are owning us, if we are distracted from service and things eternal because we have too much, then we need the courage to make a change. Because there is no quick answer to how much is too much, these changes should be made with discernment born from prayer.

Finding the Grace of Enough: Tips for Simplifying Your Life

If you're ready to declutter and simplify your home, there are oodles of resources to help guide you through each step. (I share some in the Resources section in the back of the book.) This has been done so well elsewhere that I won't try to create an extensive guide to getting rid of unnecessary items, but I will offer some simple ways to move toward a path of simplicity.

Get rid of what's not essential. Walk through your home and take stock. Do you have boxes that you haven't opened for years, books you never plan to read again, clothes you keep holding on to "just in case"? Help them find a new home.

Don't purchase what's not necessary. This might mean ignoring the deals and the sales and limiting your purchases to only what you *need.* A good deal on something you don't need isn't a good deal or good stewardship. Borrow (and share) instead of buying. Borrow items from friends, seek out a hyperlocal gift economy group such as the Buy Nothing Project (more on that in chapter 9). Or just make do without.

Shop intentionally. When a purchase is necessary, be thoughtful and intentional about what you buy. Ask yourself about the company you are buying from and its ethical practices. Consider whether it's wiser to invest in something that will last forever or purchase a less expensive option. For example, once we could afford a real mattress it made far more sense to purchase one rather than replacing air mattresses every few months.

Skip Sundays. To honor the Sabbath and consider the welfare of workers, try to avoid unnecessary purchases on Sundays. If we believe that everyone should be able to set apart their Sundays for worship and family, let's not support businesses on Sundays, when they require their staff to spend the day working. Do your grocery shopping on other days and plan your purchases accordingly.

Guide children through the decluttering process. While we didn't include our young children in decisions regarding our possessions purge before our move, as they age we include them more and more in the process of simplifying their belongings. While young children might feel upset at the idea of being separated from familiar items (even items they can no longer use such as clothing that is too small), explaining that other children could use those items can help them be excited to share. Removing outgrown clothing from our youngest child's closet was a battle until she understood that those dresses and shoes would be used by someone else. Now she exuberantly boxes up her too-small items for "a cute baby who can use them."

Value experiences over things. You can minimize the clutter that is so quick to pile up in your children's closets by being very intentional about what you bring into the home. For birthdays and Christmas, prioritize experience and family time over material gifts to help keep focus on the most important things. On such special occasions, ask grandparents to gift your children with museum and zoo memberships instead of purchasing more toys for the toy box. Or plan a simple family camping trip to celebrate a birthday instead of showering your kids with more things they don't need. It's easy to forget that while all kids enjoy receiving gifts, what our children will truly treasure is time and attention from the people they love.

Cultivate Gospel generosity. The need to hoard items you *might* need in the future is far less urgent when you embrace a more biblical attitude toward possessions. Acts of the Apostles describes the Early Church's attitude toward possessions: "The community of believers was of one heart and mind, and no one claimed that any of his possessions was his own, but they had everything in common. With great power the apostles bore witness to the resurrection of the Lord Jesus, and great favor was accorded them all. There was no needy person among them, for those who owned property or houses would sell them, bring the proceeds of the sale, and put them at the feet of the apostles, and they were distributed to each according to need" (Acts 4:32–35).

Mere minimalism is an incomplete solution to our consumerism. If we ignore a deep generosity to share what we have with others and if we are unwilling to accept help in return, we have not adopted a Gospel mind-set. This description in Acts of how the Early Church viewed resources should startle us because it is so different from our cultural attitude toward possessions that emphasizes the "mine" and not the "ours."

Your stuff is taking up your time, energy, and attention. We think we need certain comforts because we are used to them, but we can also get used to simplicity. While it wasn't my dream to live without a flushing toilet for a year, it was 100 percent doable, and after a few weeks became something that we barely even thought twice about. You can get used to anything.

We have the ability to be revolutionary. The Christian life has always been countercultural, and it has never been comfortable. As Pope Benedict XVI teaches us, "Christ did not promise an easy life. Those who desire comforts have dialed the wrong number. Rather, he shows us the way to great things, the good, towards an authentic human life."[5]

Throwaway culture offers us false freedom, unlimited "choices," and distraction from lasting and eternal truths. It promises happiness but can only provide unsatisfying temporal comfort. Because we were designed for eternity, we were made for much more than the world offers. And we can start seeking it by choosing less.

3

NURTURING A WONDROUS LOVE
FOR THE LAND

We are all responsible for the protection and care of the environment. This responsibility knows no boundaries.

—Pope Benedict XVI

The second week of our new life at the farm, my phone rang. "The piglets are being born," Daniel said. I could hear the excitement in his voice. "Bring the kids up to see!" The kids and I were waking up from a much-needed nap. After completing the Herculean task of finding matching shoes and tugging the proper pair onto the feet of each groggy child, we walked hand in hand up the farm road to the pig pen.

A handful of tiny black piglets were already wiggling around and nursing as the sow labored to bring more little ones into the world. Our kids were fascinated (although two-year-old Gwen's lack of volume control couldn't have been very helpful for the poor laboring mama pig). We crouched down to watch the miracle unfold before us along with a dozen interns and volunteers who had all stopped their work to watch in near silence (save for Gwen's screeches and exclamations). It was a moment of absolute wonder. One second a piglet was cradled in the sow's womb, the next it was sputtering and stumbling about in the sunlight. Piglet after piglet arrived. Some just a few minutes apart, others spaced more widely because they were breech and more difficult for the sow to deliver.

We watched for more than an hour: dirt, blood, work, pain, and squealing new life. Daniel and I gazed at our children's spellbound faces and then at each other, wholly understanding without words: *This is why we worked so hard to get here, so we could experience this world together.*

Benjamin called his grandparents to tell them ecstatically, "There's piglets at the farm now! We saw them get born!" Yes, we did. In the coming months we'd see the births of many more animals: piglets, calves, rabbits, and goat kids. It became a familiar scene but never ordinary. It is impossible not to feel the sacred at work when watching a birth, to approach it with awe and to lift your heart to God. It is an occasion for wonder. Living on the farm, the opportunities to be struck by the beauty and mystery of the earth abounded.

With very limited space to call our own in the farm apartment, it was natural to spend more time outdoors. We would grab our schoolbooks and head outdoors after breakfast. We'd take walks up the road to visit the dairy goats and check on the baby piglets (from afar—mama pigs are more terrifying than you might expect, and they have bona fide scary teeth to be wary of). The more time we spent outside, the more we fell in love with the land, the more we fell in love with God.

CREATED TO CONNECT

The papal encyclical *Laudato Si'* is named after a line from St. Francis of Assisi's "Canticle of the Creatures": "Praise be to you, my Lord, with all your creatures." In it, Pope Francis warns us, "We were not meant to be inundated by cement, asphalt, glass and metal, and deprived of physical contact with nature" (*LS* 44).

We experienced this disconnection from nature while we lived in Florida—especially Daniel, who left for work when it was still dark, sat in an office with artificial lighting all day without even being able to see out of a window, and then headed home in the evenings. When he returned home for dinner, I often felt the toll the day had taken on him. He was completely drained, not from pushing his body to work hard but from sitting in front of a screen all day.

We were created to have a connection to the land, to get sunshine and to dirty our hands in the soil. When we ignore and sever that connection, it can be detrimental not only to our own mental health but also to how we relate to God and to our neighbor. Yet many of us *are* deprived of physical contact with nature. As a culture, we are suffering from simply not being outside enough. As schools continue to cut down on recess, our kids spend less and less time outdoors and then often return home to more schoolwork and the siren song of screens (in fact, most of American leisure time is spent in front of the computer or TV).[1] But when we are outside and learning to love God's creation in all its glory, how can we help but seek to preserve and care for it? We honor the Creator by caring for his creation. Our awe at its beauty and the steps we take to protect it can become worship.

Viewing the world through the eyes of wonder is to have a worshipful attitude to life. To be able to wonder, we must first take the time to be attentive, to look up from our phones, and to notice God's world. Fr. Thomas Dubay explains, "To wonder is to appreciate reality in a living, vibrant way. It is to respond to being, to be fully alive. Wonder is an awesome awareness. It is a compliment to God and an enrichment of the person."[2] But in large part, we have lost that sense of enchantment with God's creation.

Pope Benedict XVI writes, "The relationship between individuals or communities and the environment ultimately stems from their relationship with God. When 'man turns his back on the Creator's plan, he provokes a disorder which has inevitable repercussions on the rest of the created order.'"[3] Inevitably this disorder causes a rupture not just within the created order but between us and God as well.

We don't have to look far to see the ugliness of that rupture. Nothing is quite so removed from the beauty of creation as modern chicken farming. Huge warehouses are filled wall-to-wall with unnaturally fat birds that can barely move. Their nearly featherless bodies sag with the weight of too much meat, often breaking their thin legs. Huge, deafeningly loud fans hum constantly, trying to pull the rank air from the facility but they aren't enough, and any worker who ventures inside is forced to wear a mask to keep out the particles of dust and sickening ammonia smell. The throwaway culture elevates profit margin as the highest good, ignoring the significance of God's land and creatures and the long-term effects on each.

Our experience at the farm showed us that another attitude toward the land is possible. As we walked up the farm road to the pastures, we saw fields of cows, sheep, and goats contentedly grazing and pigs wallowing and oinking in mud (I cannot stress how piglike pigs are. They are just such *pigs*.) The chickens were always going on escapades into the garden and into the road, keeping my children busy for hours as they tried to pet them and help them back to their designated spaces. This is, of course, a wildly different picture than one would see at your typical modern factory farm where animals are packed into tiny spaces, trapped in their own filth, and treated like living sacks of calories instead of creatures designed by God.

Past generations' gentler attitudes toward the land and greater consideration for the well-being of animals were not merely the result of primitive technology that made more exploitive practices impossible. Cultural views of family, faith, and the meaning of life gave people's existence deeper meaning and purpose than merely stripping the land of every last calorie. People were more concerned with family time or religious holidays than destroying the land for future generations in order to make a quick buck.

While considering how various practices affect the health of the land and the dignity of God's creatures is worthwhile, what's needed is a renewed concern for caring for our common home and a renewed sense of wonder to the world around us. By lifting our eyes to view God's creation as a gift deserving of our wonder, we discover that as this natural order is restored, the spiritual rupture between God and us also begins to heal.

Seeing the beauty and goodness of a field of happy cows as wildly superior to a more lucrative but disgusting factory farm is something the throwaway culture can barely comprehend. But this is why it's so important for us to fight for it.

LIVING WELL WITH GOD'S CREATURES

A quiet walk to the dairy barn in the early morning with the stars still shining isn't such a bad way to begin a new day. Especially if it's followed by resting your cheek against the side of a warm goat with the rhythm of milking while your spouse handles breakfast for your little wild monkeys. And it's hard to walk back down the farm road as the sunrise begins and not feel a deep love for the land and the animals on it, crazy goat antics and all (they must think kicking over milking pails is just *hilarious*).

There is a certain affection and love for the creatures and land that emerges when you feel an ownership for them. I learned this by seeing the care we all took of the animals on the farm, and particularly in my son's adoration of a particular farm cat. We called him Eddy because his domain was around the Education Building that housed the office space as well as retail lobby and communal eating space. Eddy was an excellent mouser (for which I was grateful, since fighting rodents in our apartment was an ongoing problem).

Unfortunately Eddy was not a good pet and 100 percent not interested in being friends. He didn't want to be touched, especially not by eager children whose "love" was more like suffocation. His hissing and snarls would precede scratches and bites. The girls quickly learned to give Eddy a wide berth, but Benjamin was not to be deterred. He *loved* Eddy and bore the marks of his affection with pride. He would defend Eddy as "the *best* cat" and spent many hours looking for or talking to the animal and considering ways to make Eddy happier. Perhaps it's a silly example, but it taught me that when you consider something to be your own, you will defend it, care for it, and love it. What if we could remember that we *all* hold the responsibility to care for our common home? Would we become nurturers and shepherds instead of exploiters and consumers?

FIND THE JOY OF ST. FRANCIS

We can find great insight into a rightly ordered view of creation care by looking at St. Francis of Assisi. Unfortunately some Christians dismiss St. Francis as merely a statue of a guy feeding the birds—a reflection of sentimental hippie earth worship. But let's take a minute to consider this saint whom our current pontiff honors with his chosen name.

While it is true that St. Francis loved animals, his life was so much more than that—as is the Franciscan order that bears his name. From the beginning St. Francis fought, according to G. K. Chesterton, to reaffirm "the Incarnation, by bringing God back to earth."[4] God's sacrifice of becoming man has significance for how we see the world, and St. Francis knew it.

St. Francis wasn't filled with joy because he was getting lots of sunshine and felt at one with nature in some

New Agey way. St. Francis was joyful because he was so filled with the love of Christ that he aimed for his every act to speak to the reality of that love, including care and awe for his Savior's world and delight in his creatures. As Christians, we should not seek to preserve the world out of an attraction to watered-down New Age spirituality but because we love its Creator, because God became man in this world and his very steps make it enchanted by the Divine. Care for his earth is our spiritual responsibility, our privilege, and if embraced, our great joy.

CREATION CARE FOUNDED IN FAITH (AND ST. FRANCIS)

St. John Paul II warns, "The earth will not continue to offer its harvest, except with *faithful stewardship*. We cannot say we love the land and then take steps to destroy it for use by future generations."[5] Yet environmental consciousness or a plea for creation care is often written off as so much political grandstanding. This is a grave mistake. Creation care is a concern that transcends political affiliation or party platform.

The rise of popular environmentalism coincided with the realization that we are capable of destroying our world and that we need to preserve it for our survival and that of our children. But the Catholic tradition has always taught that God made the world and that his goodness is reflected in creation. It follows that his handiwork should be treated with respect. We bear responsibility for its care, as God makes clear in the first chapter of the book of Genesis when he gives human beings dominion over his creation: "Let us make human beings in our image, after our likeness. Let them have dominion over the fish of the sea, the birds of the air, the tame animals, all the wild animals, and all the creatures that crawl on the earth" (Gn 1:26).

A Catholic theology of creation both predates and is superior to secular environmentalism. While secular environmentalism can give voice to issues such as endangered species or environments, it cannot answer *why* we should value preserving them. Christians, on the other hand, can say with confidence that by their very existence, God's creatures and the wonders of the earth give him praise. With the knowledge of who the Creator is and the revelations he has given us about his character, we have a solid theological foundation to discuss the common good and how we ought to act.

How do we begin to make real change regarding the care of creation? While I wish it were as simple as everyone recycling, it's not. The most wide-reaching problems are the result of the exploitative practices of corporations and governments, something most of us are not in control of. Yet that doesn't mean what we do isn't meaningful. We can seek to become reunited with the various aspects of God's creation that St. Francis referred to lovingly as his brothers and sisters in the "Canticle of the Creatures." Care of creation certainly doesn't require moving to a farm, but it does require intentionality, sacrifice, and attention in a world that prioritizes selfishness, convenience, and distraction. Such a reorientation honors God's design for human beings, their relationship with each other, and his world. Perhaps the best way to motivate these changes is to allow ourselves to fall in love with God's creation.

REDISCOVERING GOD'S BOUNTIFUL CREATION

With new live-in volunteers and interns moving to the farm every few months, it's fascinating to see, along with the challenges of this unusual life, the grounding that they experience by working outside in the earth. There is something satisfying about getting your hands dirty planting in the garden. When alumni come to visit the farm, they often consider their months there as some of the happiest of their lives. Perhaps even if you've never gardened in your life, you can sympathize with the experience of peace that comes from connecting with God's creation: a beautiful hike, an evening in the woods sitting by a campfire, a day at the beach. How can you bring reconnection to creation and the joy that accompanies it into your own life?

There are many practical ways to follow in the footsteps of St. Francis and to delight in God's creation. The Holy Father exhorts us to undertake "little daily actions" that honor the earth and its Creator, reminding us that "reusing something instead of immediately discarding it, when done for the right reasons, can be an act of love which expresses our own dignity" (LS 211).

Reusing an item sounds like such a simple, small act, but by refusing to participate in throwaway culture in little ways, we are not merely adhering to arbitrary rules of liberal environmentalism but rather loving and honoring our fellow man (and ourselves) as God intended us to be—as nurturers rather than exploiters.

There are no easy answers to the complex problems that our world faces. Our attempts to honor God through our love for his creation will not all look the same. The Holy Father reminds us that "all of us can cooperate as instruments of God for the care of creation, each according to his or her own culture, experience, involvements and talents" (LS 14).

How we live out our responsibilities will vary from person to person and from family to family. We must be cautious not to fall into anxiety or despair or to seek "solutions" such as population control that merely put bandages on problems at the risk of damaging human dignity. God has created the world for us. He has designed it to sustain us, and we are meant to live here and be fruitful. We need not act out of fear but out of love. Many of the practical actions we can undertake to preserve our world are the same actions we would take to simply be good stewards of the resources we are given and to live frugally.

RETURN TO FRUGAL LIVING

Frugality was practiced with intentionality by my grand-parents' generation and in some cases was passed down to my parents' generation and my own. The connection to the land, however, was slowly lost as the social struc-ture of those generations changed and as they transitioned away from living on the farm to urban life. This newfound mobility was often necessary in order to find work, but it also separated them from family and connection to the land they inhabited.

My mother, for example, remembers helping my great-grandmother pick out and prepare a chicken from her flock for dinner. But my grandparents left their com-munity after joining the military and did not continue those traditions that kept them rooted in place and tuned in to creation. Somewhere between my grandparents and *their* parents was the age of Victory gardens, when it was neces-sary to "use it up, wear it out, make it do, or do without." This kind of intentional living and refusal to be wasteful ended with that generation and was never recovered in American culture on a grand scale. But by taking a look to the past and to what's necessary for our world today, we can take up this mantle of responsibility for our part in God's creation. We can begin incorporating these little daily actions or habits that can help us reconnect with the earth and help us preserve it.

Finding the Grace of Enough:
Tips for Reconnecting with and Preserving the Earth

So let's get down to the nitty-gritty. In *Laudato Si'*, Pope Francis offers specific ideas of what the faithful can do to help care for the earth and reduce their consumption. He specifies things such as using public transportation; using less paper, plastic, water, and electricity; recycling; and avoiding food waste (see *LS* 211). Can you carpool more often? Turn off lights when you're not in a room? Turn up the thermostat a couple degrees in the summer and the heater down a couple degrees in the winter? Most of us can make progress in these areas with a bit of intentionality.

Give yourself the space and time to see the world around you with awe and wonder. Simply go for a walk outside, stop to watch a sunset, have a picnic, or otherwise enjoy the outdoors. You can further reconnect your life with nature by gardening and being involved in producing the food on your plate (see chapter 6 for much more on this topic).

Commit to doing what you can. Most households can reduce damage to the environment by making small but significant choices, such as being intentional about what is thrown away. As someone who is not naturally organized, I've needed time to get in the habit of carefully planning meals to avoid food waste and dealing intentionally with what's left over. Committing to eating your leftovers has the silver lining of less meal prep and saving money!

Don't be discouraged when you can't do "the perfect thing." Budget concerns, time restraints, and other challenges might make it impossible to always do the perfect thing for the environment. Don't let this keep you from making small positive changes. Your grocery budget might not allow you to always purchase meat from a local farmer, for instance. Instead of getting discouraged that this possibility is out of reach, consider what small steps you can take: eat an extra vegetarian meal each week, avoid purchasing meat from factory farms for one week out of each month, or other such improvements. God knows the challenges your family faces. All he asks is for faithfulness—do what you can when you can.

Set yourself up for success. Our experience at the farm really helped me become familiar with composting, recycling, and reducing food waste. It taught me that when there's a system in place, it's not hard to be thoughtful about sorting refuse. Now at our house we keep a bowl on the counter for compostable items such as food scraps, paper products, coffee grounds, and egg shells. It's no longer useless trash. Our nine-year-old takes the bowl outside to the compost heap to be used down the road to improve our garden soil. We sort the recyclables from what should go in the trash can. It only takes a minute (composting really isn't as complicated as it sounds, I promise). Be inspired by G. K. Chesterton's observation: "If a man could undertake to make use of all the things in his dustbin, he would be a broader genius than Shakespeare."[6]

Don't give up! The little daily actions Pope Francis recommends will help us cultivate the virtue of love for God and his creation. I often lose perspective on this and see these actions as merely tiny inconveniences. Do I really want to clean out that peanut butter jar so that it can be recycled? Is it really worthwhile to keep the house warmer in summer and colder in winter than is comfortable? Wouldn't it be easier if we had a second car? Isn't it all just a drop in the bucket? Will my actions actually affect anything at all?

But if I can remember that these little sacrifices are of great value to God because they show him that I love him enough to love the world he made and my fellow man, the inconveniences can become something beautiful and I am able to be more faithful. I'm encouraged by this quote (often attributed to St. Teresa of Calcutta): "Wash the plate not because it is dirty nor because you are told to wash it, but because you love the person who will use it next."

We could also say, "Care for God's world not because you need its resources but because you love the God who created it and the people who come after you and share it as our common home."

Consider how your household can undertake these challenges. Can you reduce food waste? Can you live with just one vehicle? Can you switch to cloth from paper products? Can you buy secondhand items? The simple habits we decide to take can be nurtured into acts of love.

Vote with your wallet. When we buy meat from factory farms that go against the dignity of the animal, we are okaying those practices. When we buy clothes that were produced unethically or purchase produce that was picked by those who were not given a living wage, we are proclaiming that we support those methods.

Now, I don't present myself as any sort of model for perfectly ethical purchases. We stop for fast food on road trips. I don't check the origins of every item of clothing we have and the companies that produced them. One could go crazy attempting to be perfect in one's purchases. But we can all make an effort to become more educated about our purchases and little by little shift our support to companies and products we truly believe in. Embrace small practical sacrifices, but more importantly, seek a change of heart, a change in perspective that acknowledges our responsibility to God's beautiful, splendid world.

Our endeavors to care for God's creation will look different according to the variety of our experiences and life situations, but we can all make small strides and sacrifices out of love. What the throwaway culture offers us is a lie that will never satisfy, because we were created for so much more than to be consumers of comfort and exploiters of creation. The loss of creature comforts and the inconveniences we accept when we take up the Cross should not deter us.

We were made for greatness! Part of that greatness includes fiercely protecting creation out of love and respect for the Creator. This attitude is born from *attention*—the attention needed to see the world around us with wonder, to seek beauty, and to offer gratitude to God for his creation. One of my favorite lines from *Laudato Si'* is "Rather than a problem to be solved, the world is a joyful mystery to be contemplated with gladness and praise" (*LS* 12). We are not called to merely check off a list but rather to have new eyes that can see the joyful mystery before us.

4

Rediscovering Beauty by
Attending to the Transcendent

The terrible thing is that beauty is not only fearful
but also mysterious. Here the devil is struggling with
God, and the battlefield is the human heart.
—Fyodor Dostoevsky, *The Brothers Karamazov*

"Can we take a walk up the farm road to enjoy the remains
of the day?" my four-year-old daughter, Lucy, asked hope-
fully. My mom taught her that charming phrase, and Lucy
loves to use it whenever she wants to watch the sun set.

Of all our kids, Lucy is the one with an eye for beauty.
She is the builder of fairy houses, maker of elaborate birthday cards, and collector of especially fine leaves and rocks.
She loves art, music, flowers, and starlight. Her appreciation
for beautiful things has forced me to stop and enjoy beauty
along with her. On this particular night the sunset was
vibrant pink and orange against a sea of blue. We admired
the view until the mosquitos began their evening attack,
forcing us to return to our little apartment for bedtime.

The world is God's handiwork. When we stand in awe
of his creation, we worship and honor the Creator. It's my

children who teach me to do this. Their enthusiasm and joy in the world around them is contagious. The delight they take in the sunflowers that cover the farm in the summertime cannot be squelched by the oppressive Texas heat that arrives in May and lingers into October. Their awe at sunsets, their careful commitment to finding the best bluebonnets and Indian paintbrushes for bouquets, and their adventurous tree-climbing challenge me to open my eyes to the beauty of God's world.

Whether it's "Look at this tiny green spider!" or "See how the cottonwood tree drops these fluffy white things that float?" or "Let's see if there's any more of the yellow flowers in the meadow!"—their voices remind me, "Pay attention! Look at the world God has created out of love for you."

When we allow ourselves to notice God's creation, we see his fingerprints everywhere. Our wonder and attention to the beauty of the world point us to its Creator. There is something gloriously human about stopping to appreciate beauty, such as watching the sun set. Taking in beauty cannot provide any monetary compensation, and it won't further your career. The experience is simply to be *enjoyed*. When the solar eclipse of 2017 was quickly approaching, a news article circulated about how much it would cost the American economy to have so many people watching and missing a couple of hours in the office. What a twisted view of experiencing a rare natural phenomenon, a thing of beauty! Stopping in the midst of the busyness of life to appreciate beauty is a practice that changes our perspective from that of throwaway culture's insatiable consumption to a posture of joy and gratitude ordered toward the transcendent.

We are designed to love truth, beauty, and goodness, which are attributes of God. Throwaway culture fights against this natural desire. Yet, while truth and goodness have been largely abandoned, the longing for beauty still lingers. We don't want to be told what to believe or how to live our lives. The call of truth and goodness is becoming quiet as a whisper, but the desire for beauty remains strong, no matter how warped our palates for it have become. It persists as a language that most can still comprehend.

THE QUEST FOR AUTHENTIC BEAUTY

On the farm, we were surrounded by beauty: the long rows of the market garden, the sunflowers that volunteered blooms everywhere we looked, pastures covered in clover blossoms and gently swaying rye. It was easy to feed our souls on the world around us that pointed us toward the Creator. St. Augustine touches on this when he writes that the earth, the sea, and the air tell us, "'Here we are, look; we're beautiful.' Their beauty is their confession. Who made these beautiful changeable things, if not one who is beautiful and unchangeable?"[1]

Beauty orients us to God, but it isn't only found in nature and rural life, of course. It can also be the result of the works of our hands, our art. Human beings are designed by God to seek and create beauty whether on a country farm or in Brooklyn. We are made to undertake the task of what J. R. R. Tolkien calls "sub-creation," a practice by which we use imagination and art to build a secondary world that reflects God's creation of our world. This can take the form of farming the soil of God's earth, painting with dyes made from the plants he created, singing a song with the voice he endowed us with, or writing a story with the imagination he placed within us. When we embrace this role of sub-creator, we can contribute to the beauty of God's world.

While throwaway culture dismisses beauty as of secondary importance or even as so subjective it is unknowable, the Christian tradition maintains that aesthetics *are* spiritually significant. Beauty can draw us to God. In fact, a study done in the United Kingdom demonstrated that visiting a church or cathedral was the catalyst for conversion for 13 percent of Christian teenagers and that beauty of sacred space was a more powerful draw than the programs specifically designed to attract youth to the faith.[2] That a beautiful church would ignite a spark that draws young people to begin life in Christ emphasizes the importance of aesthetics to the human soul. We are drawn to beauty!

One haunting recent example of Western disregard for the value of sacred beauty, so prevalent in throwaway culture, is the January 2018 destruction of the stunning Church of St. Lambertus in the western German village of Immerath. The entire village was demolished to make way for a new coal mine. The lovely nineteenth-century cathedral was destroyed to build a new space of worship for mammon. Watching the video of the demolition equipment tearing down the stones of the church was gut-wrenching. Yet the beautiful building was holding back the hand of "progress" and so was sacrificed to throwaway culture.

Fighting for beauty is one of the most essential battles of our time, one that you might think we're losing after a quick glance at modern architecture's monstrosities. But we are still drawn to beautiful things, despite all the movements promoting the drab and the brutal. Our office buildings may look like prisons ("If it's functional, efficient, and productive, why does it need to be beautiful?" the throwaway culture would say) but marketers are aware that the beauty of nature and the human form are essential for drawing us in. We are wired for it. And I think an appreciation for beauty is having a rebirth. Millennials, for instance, are often mocked for their focus on aesthetics. This focus can certainly degenerate into condescension: film snobbery, indie music buffs, weird art nuts hanging pictures by obscure artists in their hipster apartments (artists you've never heard of, of course). The dismissal of this obsession with superficial aesthetics is warranted if millennials refuse to drink anything but craft beer or claim that *Northanger Abbey* was really Jane Austen's best before she "sold out" (eye roll). But while it *can* be twisted into a pointless snobbish aestheticism, a love for beauty and appreciation for things beyond mainstream pop culture is a good sign in a throwaway culture that cannot understand the value of anything beyond its ability to build wealth.

So despite its flaws, I think the hipster stereotype actually points to a reason to hope: even after several generations surrounded by ugliness, we simply can't stop loving beauty. While hipster subculture might still be a world away from an authentic quest for beauty, it's an improvement from a complacency in the face of ugliness. It means that we have not completely lost our connection to the transcendent. It's a refusal to give in to despair even when what humanity has done to the world is ugly, drab, or even horrifying. Anyone, millennial or otherwise, can participate in the revolutionary act of fighting for the transcendent in daily life. It's something our world desperately needs.

This innate desire for beauty is part of what makes us human, ultimately pointing us to the transcendent. For this reason, Bishop Robert Barron claims that perhaps the best place to start in evangelizing is to share the beauty of the faith so that its goodness and truth can be understood: "First the beautiful, then the good, then the true."[3] Visual artists, architects, musicians, writers, educators, filmmakers, and every one of us carry the huge responsibility of pouring beauty into the cultural imagination.

Several years ago, a dear friend started an arts program for underprivileged children. When I asked her what motivated her to create this nonprofit she explained she was inspired by an art class that convinced her that beauty was essential to the human experience. She wanted to offer something that would help children to both see and create beauty. "Because of the housing and schools that make up the bulk of their daily environment, it's possible that these kids spend an entire day without seeing something that is aesthetically beautiful," she explained. "How can we expect human beings to thrive without beauty? Isn't it just as essential as other things necessary for human life?"

Pope Benedict XVI would agree with her. Beauty should not be viewed as a luxury for a few but as essential for all. At the dedication of the beautiful Sagrada Familia basilica in Barcelona, he argued that "beauty is one of mankind's greatest needs; it is the root from which the branches of our peace and the fruits of our hope come forth. Beauty also reveals God because . . . a work of beauty is pure gratuity; it calls us to freedom and draws us away from selfishness."[4] Seeking beauty is an antidote to narcissism because we must look outward to stand in awe. It directs us to God by drawing us out of ourselves to seek the Creator of all beauty.

The Sagrada Familia itself is an example of a long fight for beauty. With its construction relying on private donations and having been interrupted by the Spanish Civil War, the basilica is still incomplete 135 years after breaking ground. But its upcoming completion in the 2020s will reveal a sight that with its intricate spires literally points straight to God.

EVANGELIZING BEAUTY

Before becoming Catholic, we were "church hunting" during our college years, trying out what felt like a hundred different congregations. One Sunday we visited a church that catered to college students. We sat through Coldplay music videos before the house lights went down and a band started playing so loud we couldn't hear ourselves sing and the blinding stage lights flashed in our faces. Afterward the pastor gave a sermon about one of his favorite movies. The band played a few more songs and then it was over. We walked out of the dark church into the sunny parking lot feeling as if we had just emerged from a bad nightclub experience.

While this model of catering to a specific age demographic by providing worship that is consistent with the spirit of the times is widespread (and not just in Protestant churches), this model will ultimately fail to satisfy us. This is particularly true of millennials who have grown up in a world that's constantly trying to sell us something. We know when we are being marketed to and we're not interested in second-rate versions of popular culture. When we can go to a concert with an excellent band at a local club and talk about movies with our friends on Saturday night, why would we bother getting up early on Sunday morning for more of the same? The draw of entering sacred space for liturgy and sacraments is that it's unlike anything we can experience elsewhere, not because it's just like what we do with our friends at the local bar.

The Church has so much to offer that must not be swept away in a misguided attempt to be "relevant." It's transcendence that we crave. After all, what could be more relevant than an encounter with the Divine? The human heart desires something beyond the comfortable and familiar. We may feel comfortable in a coffee shop, but that doesn't mean our worship should be modeled after one. Perhaps we need to be *un*comfortable in our worship, drawn out of ourselves, woken up by the beauty of our faith and our tradition.

After decades of trying to offer comfort and familiarity, Christian sensibilities are once again turning toward the transcendent. Even Protestant Christian denominations are rediscovering ancient forms of prayer and embracing the rhythms of the liturgical year in their worship. In Catholic parishes, younger generations are insisting upon recovering the beauty of their faith and traditions. For those who grew up attending Mass in the iconoclastic architecture of the 1970s, often paired with unfortunate liturgical decisions, the aesthetic could hardly get worse. But this lack of physical beauty in the sacred space has not crushed the desire for it. In fact, quite the opposite.

When we first moved to the farm in 2015, the sanctuary of St. Peter's Catholic Student Center at Baylor University was—to say it charitably—disappointing aesthetically. But over the past couple of years of attending Mass there, we've watched recent renovations to the space reveal the richness of an artistic tradition of beauty. The tabernacle was brought back to the center of the church, a stunning new altarpiece was installed, and beautiful art was added to the formerly whitewashed walls. Waco's Latin Mass community finds its home there, and it's interesting that this more traditional rite is attended by students in addition to young families and older adults.

Other traditional liturgical communities are also full of young parishioners, not just the sixty-plus crowd. There is an undeniable youthful push for liturgical and architectural beauty.

Admittedly not every recently built church is a demonstration of this recovery of aesthetics. However, this reconnection to tradition and beauty by the younger generations is not a lone anecdote but a symptom of the deep thirst for beauty that has been left unsatisfied for decades. Recently built churches (such as the glorious new cathedral in Raleigh, North Carolina) are more likely to be grounded in traditionally beautiful Christian architecture than sacred buildings built fifty years ago. We want our sacred spaces to offer something not of this world or the spirit of the age but otherworldly beauty—pointing to the supernatural. The long-unsatisfied desire for beauty is beginning to change the landscape.

HOW BEAUTY DREW ME HOME

This attraction to the beauty of the faith is part of my own story of conversion. Long before I became Catholic, I had fallen in love with the beauty of the Church. Growing up Protestant in the Bible Belt, I didn't yet believe that the Church could hold the fullness of truth, but the art, music,

architecture, prayers, liturgy, and traditions were all so rich
and beautiful that I couldn't help myself. I had to know
more about the Church. Its beauty drew me like a magnet,
its truth convinced me, and its goodness began flowing
into my life. The true, the good, and the beautiful—these
are the things human beings are wired for. The things we
are created to love.

When we were still attending a Baptist church, I found
myself drawn to the beauty of the Rosary before I was comfortable asking for our Lady's intercession. Even as a Protestant, attending a beautiful Mass at a basilica where I was
attending a nearby conference brought me to tears—not
because it was familiar or made me feel comfortable (it was
unfamiliar and I felt decidedly uncomfortable and out of
place) but because the Church offered something vast and
rich and completely unlike anything I had ever known or
experienced.

The Russian writer Fyodor Dostoevsky claims "beauty
will save the world."[5] Aesthetics matter. The beauty of the
liturgy, the quality of the art, and music of the tradition—all
of it matters *immensely*. We cannot brush it off as insignificant or attempt to replace the transcendent with shallow
entertainment. Rather, we must offer an alternative to the
spirit of the age by pointing to the supernatural through
beauty: the solemn beauty of the *Kyrie eleison* ("Lord, have
mercy") sung by the cantor; the startling beauty of a crucifix, the image of the grotesque and scandalous love of
God for humanity; the beauty of an icon of our Lady with
eyes that carry sorrow and mercy and a womb that carried
God himself; the beauty of an ancient hymn such as "Let
All Mortal Flesh Keep Silence" that makes you shiver; the
beauty of Michelangelo's *Pietà*.

I believe the Church offers this salvation, this beauty
that shines through the Church in a million ways—including those things that may not be superficially attractive. For example, the poor, twisted feet of St. Teresa of

Calcutta—misshapen from serving for decades while wearing shoes no one else wanted—were not pretty and yet they
are beautiful as an image of the blessed feet that bring the
Good News of the Gospel. Indeed, the Christian tradition
can offer the beauty that will save the world.

Finding the Grace of Enough: Tips for Embracing Beauty

If beauty matters so much, how do we seek beauty in our
daily lives in ways that benefit our souls? I think the first
step is to shift our perspective. We have to make *space* for
beauty. We may be so saturated in the throwaway culture
that we tend to attach a price tag to each of our actions
every hour of the day. But if we see through those consumerist lenses we will fail to seek the transcendent. In *Laudato
Si'*, Pope Francis writes that a recognition and appreciation
for beauty rejects "self-interested pragmatism." The Holy
Father explains that "if someone has not learned to stop and
admire something beautiful, we should not be surprised
if he or she treats everything as an object to be used and
abused without scruple" (*LS* 215). We must learn to value
what's eternal and transcendent in order to extricate ourselves from the consumerist attitude that would turn us
away from a right relationship with God, his creation, and
our fellow man.

   *Create beauty in your daily environment for yourself and
others.* You can seek to make your home a place of beauty.
This does not mean that you need to jump in the car and
fill it with new home goods purchases. (Remember we're
not trying to find yet another way to employ consumerism
in our lives.) Seeking beauty in the home does not have to
cost money. It can be as simple as growing flowers in a pot
on your porch and placing them in a vase in the center of
your table. And it is so much easier to have space in our
hearts for beauty if we have embraced living with less and
our homes are not overflowing with unnecessary items
sucking up our energy and mental space.

In an effort to make our home a place of beauty (on a shoestring budget), Daniel and I have prioritized sacred art. Slowly over the years we've been accumulating beautiful prints and icons. We often give them as birthday or Christmas gifts to each other. I love that in our living and dining rooms the walls are filled with images of our Lord, our Lady, and the saints. These pockets of sacred art remind us of our Catholic family culture but also of the beauty of our faith that our daily lives should seek to imitate. By surrounding ourselves with beauty (art, music, and the like), we are changing our hearts.

Seek to find beauty in your daily activities. This is something I am not particularly hardwired for. I am not artistically inclined, and I don't have a crafty bone in my body (my family members can attest to this). I am a failure at interior decorating and my daily life is often like the inside of my head and my handwriting—a bit of a mess. But seeking to appreciate beauty doesn't mean maintaining a perfect home or producing stunning artwork. It can be possible by recognizing the beauty and value of small things such as a garden bed, a well-steeped cup of tea, or a beautifully baked loaf of bread. The sacred touches the everyday if we have eyes to see.

English writer and famous Catholic convert G. K. Chesterton notes that "if a thing is worth doing, it is worth doing badly."[6] I keep this in mind because I am *not* one of those people who seems to be able to beautify everything she touches. I will never achieve Pinterest-worthy homemaking or professional-quality plating for a meal. My natural bent is to slop some soup into bowls and hope it's edible. But with a husband who is a culinary mastermind, I've come to appreciate the beauty of a plate prepared by Daniel, with his artistic eye. To take the time and intentionality to make small things in life beautiful, even if it's just adding chopped cilantro to the top of the enchiladas, can be life changing.

Remove things that harm your soul with their ugliness. If we truly believe that beauty can lift the heart to God, then it follows that by surrounding ourselves with ugliness, our spiritual life will suffer. Is the media we are consuming beautiful? By this, I don't mean is it without conflict, violence, pain, or scandal. I can't imagine many things better for one's soul than Flannery O'Connor's Southern gothic writings, for example, which are full of the grotesque and shocking, because there is a transcendent beauty to her portrayal of the unforeseen workings of grace.

Neither does "avoiding ugliness" mean shunning high-quality storytelling merely because the tale includes sin or fallen man (I'm thinking something such as the unsurpassed series *Mad Men* here)—all good stories do, including the Holy Scriptures. But the mindless, trashy media and distractions that we use to drown out the still small voice do us no favors. Pope Francis warns us that the "words of love" cannot be heard "amid constant noise, interminable and nerve-wracking distractions, or the cult of appearances" (*LS* 225). His words are convicting to me with my penchant to seek distraction over the truly worthwhile. Do we allow the ugly noise of life to drown out beauty and contemplation? Is there any peace and quiet to our days that allows us to be open to receive beauty and listen to God's words of love he desires to speak to us in his creation and the handiwork of his creatures?

My fellow parents of small children are probably giving me a resounding "No! There is no peace and quiet to my days!" I feel your pain because they're certainly hard to come by in our home too. There's a rowdy hum of life within our walls. My home full of small children does not feel like a monastery, nor should I expect it to. But does that mean I'm doomed to have no peace or beauty there? I don't think so.

To the parents out there, we have the weighty privilege of forming the imaginations of our children to be full of beauty. It's crucial that regardless of our schooling choices for them (traditional brick-and-mortar or homeschooling), we undertake this task with conviction. We have the opportunity to surround our children with music, stories, art, and nature that prepare them to connect with the beauty of their faith. We can weave these things into our days. The music we listen to, the art on our walls, the films we watch together, the books we read aloud are powerful influences. While I certainly don't think it's necessary to weed out every single pop culture influence (and growing up in a conservative homeschooling community, I've seen it go terribly awry in many cases when pop culture is seen as the forbidden fruit), I do think it's important for the primary influences in our homes to be ones of true beauty. Tolkien and Bach formed me during my childhood when if left to my own devices I would have stuck with *The Baby-Sitters Club* and mid-'90s pop. There is plenty of the ugly and banal that our kids will encounter in life. Don't tire of fighting for the beautiful to fill your child's world.

Be intentional about encouraging those who create beauty. Support gifted artisans, writers, poets, and craftsmen. Get involved in your parish to help beautify your sacred spaces and seek truly beautiful liturgy. The Holy Mass gives us the chance to encounter the most beautiful of all beings and the Eucharist gives us the chance to offer this beauty back to God. Every time the priest elevates the host, I think of the line from the band MewithoutYou about holding up a mirror: "Lord, I could never show you anything as beautiful as you."[7]

In *The Weight of Glory*, Christian writer C. S. Lewis writes, "We do not want merely to see beauty, though, God knows, even that is bounty enough. We want something else which can hardly be put into words—to be united with the beauty we see, to pass into it, to receive it into ourselves, to bathe in it, to become part of it."[8] We long for beauty because we long for God. If we take a step toward

appreciating beauty, we are coming closer to union with
God. The longing for beauty is most fully satisfied in the
Eucharist when we truly can "receive [beauty] into ourselves," as Lewis says. The commitment to seek beauty is
not of secondary importance; it is a revolutionary act in
a throwaway culture that has ceased to pursue the transcendent. If the world is literally bulldozing cathedrals,
we have to be actively building beauty into the world. By
seeking beauty, we are led back to the ultimate embodi-
ment of beauty, and can point others back to him as well.
By turning us back toward the Savior, beauty can indeed
save the world.

5

Making Home a Priority, a School of Love

> Our kitchens and other eating places more and more resemble filling stations, as our homes more and more resemble motels.
>
> —Wendell Berry, *The Art of the Commonplace*

I woke to the scent of sautéing garlic and onions and shuffled out of the small bedroom, barely big enough for our mattress and a single dresser, in our new space at the farm. It only took six steps to walk to the kitchen on the other side of the apartment. Our early-rising kids were bouncing around the table as Daniel cooked a frittata, and our four-year-old deep sleeper was still tucked under her covers in the kids' room. She stumbled out of bed just in time to eat as Daniel read the daily Mass readings before leaving to start work with the livestock for the day.

I can't believe we get to see him again at lunchtime, I thought to myself. Our dream of eating three meals a day as a family had arrived. Daniel was never completely "off the clock," since he was on call for pigs that escaped from their pens, mama goats that needed help during delivery, or any other farm emergency. Yet we got to see much more of him than ever before.

Raising little ones in Florida had been tough, even with helpful extended family nearby to pitch in during emergencies. Surviving until dinnertime when Daniel was away for ten hours a day had been hard on my mental health. I experienced extreme morning sickness during all three trimesters of my pregnancies due to hyperemesis gravidarum, a condition that requires strong prescription drugs just so I can keep water down. Having three of our kids in quick succession pushed me to the brink of what I could handle.

While I was out of commission during pregnancy, Daniel handled all the food prep and cleaning. (There's no way I could have tackled that with my condition.) But he couldn't stay home all day, every day. Somebody needed to work so we could pay our bills, and he would often leave before sunrise and not get home until dark. Home became the place where he slept.

Being at the farm and having him nearby during the day was a dream come true. He was certainly busy keeping animals fed and watered and building and maintaining fences (there was a running joke at the farm that the livestock internship was really a fence-building internship), but he was often just a few yards away. Benjamin, our oldest, would sometimes join him to feed the chickens or check the cows' water. I would take the kids on long walks up the farm road to reconnect with Daniel during the day. With all of us staying close to home with a common project, we were bonding as a family in a new, beautiful way.

A lot of our friends would comment on all the sacrifices we made to leave our former life and begin again at the farm: selling our house in Florida, moving across the country, no flushing toilets, tiny living space, huge pay cut, and so on. But for us, life had gotten so much better for our family that it really didn't *feel* sacrificial at all. It felt as if we were finally thriving because we were finally all together doing work we loved.

THE HOTEL HOME

With family members often going in many directions during the day, home as the center of life can feel impossible. Due to our current economic climate, many American families need dual incomes that often require both parents to work outside the home while the children spend significant portions of their days at school, followed by extracurricular activities. Employment, education, and enrichment are all blessings, indeed. But it can be challenging to make the home central and not treat it like a hotel, showing up exhausted in the evening to sleep and then packing up and doing the whole thing all over again the next day. In one of my favorite essays, farmer and writer Wendell Berry observes, "The modern household is the place where the consumptive couple do their consuming. Nothing productive is done there."[1]

Home has become the place where we watch TV. It's where we sleep after a long day. But it rarely serves as the center of life anymore. Whether it's the deeply ingrained Protestant work ethic urging us to be constantly productive or the throwaway culture keeping us from seeing value in the joys of family life that have nothing to do with consuming or achieving affluence, we often need reminders to do even simple, normal things that don't have price tags.

Pope Francis urges parents to "waste time with your children."[2] While such advice should be unnecessary, this reminder convicts me every time I think about it. Have I wasted time with my children today? Often the answer is no. For those without children, you might ask yourself: Have I had a conversation with someone today that had nothing to do with work, networking, or financial gain? Did I call a family member just to connect? Meet a friend for a bite to eat just to encourage each other? What did I do today to bestow love on another human being, no strings attached?

In a capitalist society, the goal is to acquire capital. If we are not consuming, we feel a pull to make progress toward financial gains for ourselves. Anything else is seen as a luxury or waste of time. This thinking bleeds into how we guide our children as well.

Think about it. Is every minute of the day ordered toward work, from preparing children for college (so that they can become future employees) to attending to the details of our own workplace? Are we encouraging our teens to cram extracurriculars into family schedules because such activities will look great on college applications? Do we race from one activity to the next with little real enjoyment, or do we focus on spending truly valuable hours "wasting time" together? How often are we doing things that are good for our souls and our growth in love and virtue that have nothing to do with making money? Reclaiming these worthwhile facets of home life—such as the simple habit of eating dinner together—must become our goal.

LIVE TO WORK OR WORK TO LIVE?

We haven't always lived in a *Mad Men*'s world of Don Drapers and Peggy Olsons, whose work lives are disconnected from their home lives (apart from earning money to purchase things for the house). If you think of "the olden days," such as Laura Ingalls Wilder's pioneer experience, a man's work was providing for his family's home and sustenance, and that entailed working on his own land and being near his family.

So our current attitudes toward domestic matters, which regard home as little more than a family's hotel, is a relatively new one. There was a time when home was the center of not just family life but also the center of each man and woman's own life and work. A *husband* was a man who cared for his house; *husbandry* referred to the care and cultivation of crops and animals. As fathers began to leave their homes and fields to go to work first in the factories of the Industrial Revolution and later in office buildings, it greatly changed the fabric of family life.

The world has changed from the *Little House on the Prairie* days, of course. We can't all be Pa Ingalls! While pursuing careers that allow for more family time would be a positive shift, the typical couple can't just drop everything and sustain their family's livelihood by caring for their own home and land. Even after being equipped by such great training at the farm, we still need jobs to pay our mortgage that won't be covered merely by proceeds from our vegetable garden and backyard chickens.

While most families find that generating a dual income makes prioritizing home life a challenge, there have been some recent positive trends. The rise of a work-from-home lifestyle has helped some families (including mine) in their desire for more intentional home life, though this isn't the right situation (or even a possibility) for all. Of course, having fulfilling work that requires being away from home during the day isn't a bad thing, nor does this preclude anyone from having a thriving home life. In fact, some of the most home-centered families I know are comprised of two working parents who have ordered their careers and their energy toward making home and family the priority of their lives. One couple I admire makes extensive efforts to organize their schedules so that their children are with at least one parent as often as possible, even if it means working unusual shifts. While working hard to provide their children with what they need, their focus is on having a thriving family that takes precedence over employment advancement and pay scales. They seek to build a life, not merely a bank account or career accolades. Home is number one, and all other endeavors are designed to make that home life possible.

After Daniel's internship at the farm was over and he transitioned to full-time nonprofit work, we moved out of our farm apartment. Now we own a house in the middle of town. We don't get to see Daniel during his work shifts as we did when we lived at the farm, but we've tried to continue keeping home as central to our lives as possible. We have learned to live on less so that neither of us needs to work overtime. Because I can do my work from home or odd hours at coffee shops when Daniel's with the kids, we have the flexibility to arrange those hours according to our family's needs. We are thankful that we have this flexibility—not everyone does. And we are constantly tweaking our work life in order to do what's best for our family at that time. There is no one "right" way to set things up that will fit for every family. But we can all seek to restore the home as the center of life by prioritizing time we spend as a family, by cooking and eating together around the dining room table, and by centering our days and time with prayer and liturgical living that contribute to a family culture anchored in faith.

CREATING YOUR "DOMESTIC CHURCH"

The *Catechism of the Catholic Church* states, "The home is the first school of Christian life and 'a school for human enrichment' . . . [where] one learns . . . fraternal love, generous—even repeated—forgiveness, and above all divine worship in prayer and the offering of one's life" (*CCC*, 1657). Home and family are where the journey begins. While parish life certainly contributes to our spiritual growth, home is where we live out our daily devotion.

Prayer and liturgical living can keep us anchored in our faith. As our children have grown, our family prayer practices have shifted according to what works for our family at the time. There have been seasons when it feels as if prayer over meals is all that happens consistently, and other times when we are doing a daily family Rosary. Don't beat yourself up over not praying *all* the hours *and* making it to daily Mass *and and and* (insert whatever devotion you feel guilty about not doing here). Obsessing over not doing all the things perfectly can paralyze you. Make family prayer a priority and do the best you can in the season you're in. The goal is to make your home a house of prayer, not to check off a list for "perfect Catholic family." That list doesn't exist, and neither does that family you may have imagined in your head.

You can start by choosing just one devotion, such as the Rosary, and trying to add just that prayer consistently into your daily life. While a family Rosary can seem intimidating, with some patience it can become a beautiful tradition even for young children. It didn't click with our kids until a couple of years ago when we started praying it in the car when everyone was buckled in and couldn't run wild (go figure). But after plenty of practice, a family Rosary is now a special time. The kids love to grab their rosaries and lead decades.

Don't be discouraged if it doesn't go well at first. Nobody's kids sit through it perfectly on day one. If they're anything like mine, day one will definitely involve somebody crying and someone injuring a sibling with a rosary. Remember, even St. Thérèse of Lisieux had trouble praying the Rosary. She confessed, "(I am ashamed to admit it) the recitation of the Rosary is more difficult for me than the wearing of an instrument of penance."[3] So if it's not an easy devotion for you, you're in good company. Don't stress. Just let it wash over you.

A less overwhelming prayer to introduce to children is the Angelus. It's only been the past year or so that we've brought the Angelus into our home for daily prayer. Because it's traditionally said at noon, it happens in the middle of our homeschool day. I set an alarm on my phone that lets me know when it's noon, and we gather in front of our family altar to pray. This prayer is much shorter than a Rosary and a great way to re-center the day in prayer.

Speaking of a family altar, having a physical space for prayer (a "little Oratory" as Leila Marie Lawler calls it in her lovely book cowritten with David Clayton) is a truly beautiful way to center your home in prayer and remind you that the home truly is the domestic church. Our family altar is in our dining room. It's a small table (with room for our religious books underneath) with candles and a crucifix. We have most of our icons as well as our rosaries on the wall above it. It creates a place of beauty to gather and for the children (and us) to experience prayer through multiple senses: the smell of the candles, the beauty of the icons, and the sound of the words said or sung.

Another facet of transforming the home into the domestic church is the observation of the liturgical year. While practical advice about bringing the Christian year into family life could fill many books (and I include a list of my favorite resources in the back of this book), the key idea is to turn away from the busyness of modern life and the commercial calendar to live by holy time. The Church gives us a way to keep time that points us toward spiritual truths. By using this holy calendar, one of the beautiful spiritual rhythms pointing to salvation history, we walk with Christ through the year alongside the saints. It's a cycle that slowly forms us like water smoothing river rocks. If we allow the liturgical seasons to shape our homes, we have the opportunity to have our family's traditions and rhythms formed by the beauty of the Church.

The liturgical year was one facet of the Catholic faith that attracted us when we became interested in conversion. Growing up in a tradition that celebrated Christmas and Easter but neglected all other liturgical observances, we were dazzled by the richness and beauty of the Christian year when it was finally presented to us. Participating in honoring the saints, preparing our hearts through seasons of penitence, and celebrating the holy feasts has been life-giving for our family and our spiritual lives. (We elaborate on some of these celebrations in our book *Feast!*)

Observing the preparatory seasons of Advent and Lent and celebrating in festal seasons such as Christmas and Easter shouldn't be left only to the parish but should permeate our home lives as well. While the same daily tasks of work, cooking, and laundry must be completed, when we count time with the liturgical calendar our mundane tasks can be seen in the light of the sacred because our days are oriented toward eternal truths.

The goal, of course, with any of these practices is for the home to be that school of love that the *Catechism* describes, the place that guides us and prepares us for holiness. With so many distractions and pressures attempting to pull us away from the relationships, sacrifices, and spiritual practices that could help us become saints, we have to fight against the hotel-home model. Wendell Berry reminds us that despite the negative trends away from family life, "there are, however, still some married couples who understand themselves as belonging to their marriage, to each other, and to their children."[4] Those of us called to the vocation of marriage can be those families by choosing to center life around the home.

BALANCING HOME AND SERVICE

It can be easy to minimize the importance of home life. Isn't there so much work to be done out in the world? Aren't there so many hurting people? Aren't there so many people in need? Yes. But for many of us, the way we will most effectively change the world is through how we approach our home and family life.

Even Mother Teresa, now St. Teresa of Calcutta, who spent her life ministering in the world and truly changed the world through her service, believed this. When she received the Nobel Peace Prize and was asked what people can do to promote world peace, she answered, "Go home and love your family."[5] We can do our most important work by seeking to create a domestic church in a culture that sees home and family life as a waste of time. Seen in this light, praying the Rosary after enjoying a meal with your loved ones is one of the most powerful and transformative things you could ever do with your time.

Finding the Grace of Enough:
Tips for Making Home a School of Love

If the *Catechism* is right and the home is meant to be a school of love (see *CCC*, 1657), then we have to show up to attend class there sometimes, right? So how do we make this a reality in our homes? How do we shift to a perspective that seeks to honor the importance of this basic unit of love on a practical level?

Give home life the first fruits of your time and energy. Move away from thinking of home life as where you give what's left of you at the end of the day. Because the communal experience of food runs deep, one great place to start is in prioritizing family meals. Protecting mealtimes for conversation and reconnection is often the best thing we can do for family life.

There may be seasons in which work schedules or activities make weeknight family dinners impossible. If this is the case, try to find other special times to eat together. Daniel's current job involves some late afternoon and evening shifts, so breakfast and lunch are our special meals on those days. If family members are working second-shift jobs, be creative about when you can eat together or try to catch up on weekends with time around the table, grilling out or eating slowly together.

Remember that you are a valuable member of your family and community. For those who are single, you can still choose to make home your center, even if you haven't started a family. Make an extra effort to spend time with your parents and siblings, or if you live far away from your family, cultivate deep friendships, not just with other singles but also with other families in your parish. We'll discuss this in more detail in the chapter 7, but your presence in the home life of others can be a great blessing to those friends in the vocation of marriage, and vice versa. There is likely a family that is just waiting to adopt you into their home life. While I would never dismiss the unique challenges of single life or equate friendship with other families with having your own family, the relationships between single folks and families can be life-giving for both.

Remember that nurturing home life need not involve spending a lot of money. In fact, *having* time to spend as a family is often a result of intentional frugality that makes more time at home possible. Playing board games or having family movie nights requires almost no cash at all (though they are much better with popcorn!). Devoting Sundays to spending time together over good meals, reading aloud, walking in the park, riding bikes, or hiking builds up family life (as well as follows our obligation to set aside the Sabbath for rest). It never has to be elaborate.

Parents, you are enough. All children love to have time "wasted" with them; they're not hard to please. To make a day special often just requires labeling it as such and everyone will jump on board. Call the day you eat the first watermelon of the summer on your front porch "Watermelon Day," and it's an instant hit (ask me how I know). Our last Christmas season arrived during the very worst weeks of severe nausea of my fourth pregnancy. I felt terribly guilty about not being able to take the kids to do all the fun things we usually do during Christmastide and bemoaned how many days we spent on the couch just watching movies together because that was all my body could handle. I convinced myself that my children would have bad memories from that disappointing Christmas when Mom could barely get out of bed. But they found great joy in the small things we did to mark the season. I realized that I should not have been so critical of myself because while it wasn't my perfect vision for the holidays, being together as a family was really all our kids needed in order for it to feel magical. Attention and love are often all that's required to make good memories.

"Waste" time together, make your home the place where life happens, devote your family to growing together in holiness, and allow your home to be nourished with each meal you share around the table. Watch these small acts of love change the world.

PART II

RECONNECTING
WITH WHAT MAKES
US HUMAN

6

THE FIVE-HOUR DINNER: REDEEMING THE TABLE WITH SLOW FOOD

> If more of us valued food and cheer and song above
> hoarded gold, it would be a merrier world.
> —J. R. R. Tolkien, *The Hobbit*

Waco in October can be oppressively hot. I could feel the sweat trickle down my back as I sat at the wooden picnic table and watched the kids play on the rope swing right outside our apartment's kitchen window. Woodsmoke filled my nostrils from the open fire Daniel was coaxing to life, and a feeling of well-being filled my soul as some "farmies" and I sliced vegetables to grill while the sun started to set. Homeschooling can sometimes feel isolating, so laughing and talking with other grown-ups in the evening is always a welcome cap to the day.

The upside of hot and sticky October weather is that you can still harvest tomatoes and okra into early fall. We were enjoying the literal fruits of our labors. Grilled peppers, okra, onions, and squash were sizzling alongside pork chops from the farm piggies. Fresh, colorful salsa was ready to top the meat. The woodsmoke kept the mosquitos at bay as we chatted about farm news and happenings. (Yes, we still have mosquitos in October; it's penance for having such good Tex-Mex.) We hoped dinner would beat nightfall so that we could avoid clearing the picnic table in the dark.

As usual, we fell into conversation and failed to finish before daylight expired, needing flashlight apps on cell phones to find our way around. After two or three of us hand-washed the dishes inside (no dishwasher in the apartment), we joined the others around the still-crackling fire. The kids begged to roast marshmallows and went hunting for proper roasting sticks in the dark. I tried to convince my two-year-old daredevil, Gwen, to sit on my lap during the marshmallow roasting so I wouldn't have to worry about her getting burned.

Slowly the evening wound down. With bedtime long past, Daniel rounded up the six-and-under crowd, wiped off the remains of sticky marshmallow, and tucked them into bed to give me the opportunity to relax and sit by the fire.

Dinner couldn't have been fresher; the produce had still been drawing sustenance from the earth hours before. It was simply prepared and utterly superb with smoky grilled flavor. Daniel had presented each plate beautifully, drawing us together to the table. While the conversation and laughter fed our souls, the physical nourishment also had a spiritual dimension that I was rediscovering with our community at the farm.

I didn't grow up in a culinary-minded family. My great-grandmother's meals were the stuff of family legend (she even cooked for the actor Roy Rogers once). But apart from our family tradition of baking her unbeatable cream pie recipes for Thanksgiving, her gift of making culinary masterpieces did not trickle down into my immediate family.

Daniel's food history was quite different. He grew up in New Orleans, a culinary mecca, and had fallen in love with its flavors as a small child. Because his parents sometimes had church commitments in the evening (my father-in-law is a Southern Baptist minister), the family would frequently meet for dinner at restaurants to have family time after the school/work day. Some nights Daniel would cook for himself, and by his junior year of high school (when we became acquainted) he already knew his way around a kitchen and would prepare meals for friends.

I, on the other hand, was a notoriously picky eater who between the ages of five and twelve survived mostly on Eggo waffles, and who continued to refuse vegetables well into my teens. But since I knew I wanted to marry Daniel almost immediately after setting eyes on him, I was *not* going to turn up my nose at any of his meals and ruin my prospects. And lo and behold, the vegetables he made were splendid, flavorful. Our friendship, and later our romance, opened up a whole new world of food for me. I came to understand that food transcends the practical. It's not just about getting a certain number of calories to sustain your body; it's about a human experience that brings us together.

FOOD AND FRIENDSHIP: SAVORING LIFE TOGETHER

When we got married, my cooking repertoire consisted of boiling pasta, scrambling eggs, and making French toast. I counted my blessings that Daniel was skilled in the kitchen. Learning to cook was a painful and unfamiliar process for me that involved lots of tears and kitchen meltdowns. Over the years I've come to enjoy cooking as the kitchen became less of a mystery and more like a friend, but I don't have the same creative culinary spark as my husband. I stick to my tried-and-true recipes and comfort food. He embarks on culinary adventures—always perfecting, experimenting, and making the presentation more beautiful. Preparing a five-course meal for one hundred people is fun for him, while just the idea makes me want to curl up in fetal position.

Although my husband loves to spend hours cooking and serving feasts to share with friends, such evenings seldom happened when we lived in Florida. Everyone was busy—including us. Even on nights when we were ready to entertain, it could be hard to find anyone with the time to come over and join us. But life on the farm offered something different: a break from the packed schedules to spend with slower food and a built-in community to provide faces around the table.

Our move to the farm reconnected us with the joy of food. After our move, we brought back a practice we hadn't regularly experienced since our college days. We call it "the five-hour dinner." There's nothing magical about it, and there are no hard-and-fast rules. It's just cooking with friends and enjoying food and company. And there's no rush. If you do it right, it will take about five hours from beginning prep to the conversations while drying dishes. Taking that much time away from the work and worries of the world simply to eat dinner is countercultural, but it's so pleasant you won't find it sacrificial to try it every so often.

RETURN TO THE FAMILY TABLE

While I grew up in a family that ate together every night, my experience was far from the norm. It was the '80s and '90s, the era of fast food and frozen dinners. Vestiges of the "family dinner" remained in the memories of our baby boomer parents' childhoods, but few millennials experienced the table as the center of family life. The family table has been replaced by the inside of the car on the way to soccer practice or the couch in front of the TV.

Somewhere along the way we lost the sense that sharing food around the table is a simple but crucial part of the human experience. In fact, as sensory beings we are wired to care about food and connect to other people through that shared experience of eating together. This communal aspect of eating is why food allergies can feel isolating. It's why holiday cooking is so emotive and the scents and flavors of a Thanksgiving meal can draw us back to important memories. Every one of us could probably claim it's "not Thanksgiving" without such-and-such dish on the table. (For me, it's au gratin potatoes and pumpkin pie. For you, it might be cranberry sauce or sweet potato casserole with tiny marshmallows on top. No judgment.)

The physical experience of preparing, cooking, and eating together matters, but throwaway culture can't see beyond consumption. We either diminish the importance of the experience of food altogether (think frozen meals and meal replacement shakes) or we become obsessed with seeing nutrition as a scientific endeavor, compulsively breaking down our meals into calories and nutrients and losing all sense of the human connection of enjoying food. This neglect of the joy of the table results in a profound loneliness.

THE SLOW-FOOD SOLUTION

Thankfully the pendulum is swinging. As an alternative to the fast-food lifestyle, the slow food movement, which promotes local and traditional food and cooking, began in the '80s and has been growing ever since. The idea of eating things that grow near you and eating meals your great-grandparents might have eaten seems simple and not very revolutionary, but the slow food movement has become powerful and widespread, and seems even more alluring to the younger generations.

Millennials are notorious foodies. We're mocked for our elite snacks such as avocado toast and for pompously Instagramming our meals. Our love of exotic ingredients and local restaurants has made us complicit in the demise of major restaurant chains. (We've been blamed for "killing Applebee's," a charge I for one am happy to accept on

behalf of millennials everywhere.) While there's no denying that millennials are eating differently, or that this focus
on the pleasure of good food can become disordered and
turn into epicurism, I think this renewed interest in food
culture stems from something truly good: a desire to share
the experience of eating food *together*.

Many of those caught up in throwaway culture have
forgotten that food and creation are inextricably linked.
Wendell Berry reminds us that eaters "must understand
that eating takes place inescapably in the world, that it is
inescapably an agricultural act, and that how we eat deter-
mines, to a considerable extent, how the world is used."[1]
When I was learning to cook in my early twenties, I gave
no thought to the food I purchased beyond where it was
located at the grocery store. That it came from a farm somewhere was a fact buried in my subconscious; I never considered what farm, where, with what practices, harvested
by whom. None of it ever crossed my mind.

With our experiences at the farm, of course, it was
impossible to forget that our food was connected to the
land. The squash and tomatoes? Straight from the garden.
The blackberries and yogurt? Compliments of the berry
patch next to the Education Building and the dairy goats
up the road. The sausage on the table? We raised the pig
that provided it. Sure, it might be a little unnerving to hear
your two-year-old ask you to "pass the Thelma" when pork
chops are served after a favorite farm pig is butchered. But
following the life cycle of farm animals from birth to slaugh-
ter was a valuable experience for all of us.

My son raised a baby rabbit, cared for him daily, helped
butcher and skin him, and assisted in cooking the meat.
As I watched him dig into dinner that night, I realized that
another important lesson from our year on the farm was
playing out before my eyes. Because we had raised the livestock that provided the food for our table, we were doubly
thankful: grateful to God who brought us to this place and

thankful for the animal that had provided the meat—at a great price.

By the end of our year on the farm, we started cooking more vegetarian meals simply because Daniel was tired of killing animals. It's not fun work. Yet it's all too easy to forget the process when it's nicely packaged in the meat aisle at the grocery store. It's important to remember that the food we eat is connected to the earth, and that we have been called to be caretakers of God's creatures (as we discussed in chapter 3).

When we turn a blind eye to this connection, we begin to lose touch with the responsibility God gave us to be stewards of the earth. When that happens, it's only a matter of time before other problems emerge, such as injustice toward workers in the agricultural and food service industries, hoarding and waste, and unhealthy agricultural practices. To the degree that we maintain an awareness of the process by which our food comes to us, we can steel ourselves against consumerist ideas that creep into our subconscious. This means slowing down enough to enjoy what isn't quantifiable through the human connection of sharing food—and obtaining that food as close as possible from its original source.

SEASONAL EATING

Our meals at the farm were simple, made from a limited number of ingredients that were readily available. This meant sticking to what was in season. This was both a challenge and an opportunity to spark the creativity of the person who was "chef for the day," making the noontime meal. While we prepared breakfast and dinner on our own, lunch was the main meal of the day, eaten in community at the farm.

Each day the chef was in charge of creating a meal for twenty to forty (depending on how many volunteers, staff, and interns were on site that day) out of the staples in the pantry and the produce coming out of the garden. Often there were enough leftovers to enjoy a few hours later for dinner.

When the lunch bell rang, everybody stopped. Whether you were weeding in the garden, working with livestock, or fixing marketing spreadsheets, work ended promptly for the shared noontime meal. (What a contrast to my postcollege days of working through lunch at my office job and snarfing down a sandwich at my desk or even wrapping a cheese stick in a turkey slice in the midst of homeschool chaos as I was wont to do before our move to the farm.)

Meals are meant to be a *shared* experience. Stopping to make it so takes time and intentionality but reaps the rewards of human connection and community. Our great-grandparents wouldn't have questioned this practice, but we are having to relearn it. The speed of life can only increase so much until we all stand exhausted at the brink of a counterrevolution: one of a slow nurturing of relationships and traditions.

Finding the Grace of Enough:
Tips for Rediscovering the Family Table

So how do we begin chipping away at the speed of our busy days in order to slow down and get food rightly ordered in our lives?

Understand that the enjoyment of food is a human experience. The enjoyment of food transcends the physical contents of our plates (or fast-food packaging). I will be the first to admit that I'm not a purist when it comes to food. Sure, we do make an earnest attempt to grow our own produce and herbs and raise our own chickens for eggs. We try to eat local meat and support our local farmers. But I also don't say no to pregnancy cravings for Whataburger breakfast sandwiches. We regularly eat out for tacos whether the meat is local or not, and we enjoy a breakfast platter at Cracker Barrel when we're on the road. So I'm not here to judge your eating habits but rather to help you brainstorm how to put food in its proper place in your life. This involves more than simply checking off a mental list. It involves changing the way you look at and think about what you eat.

Exercise your gardening skills. One of the best ways to rewire the way you think about food is to grow some. I don't have a green thumb, but luckily I have a husband who does. If you have a yard, starting a garden is a great way to get reacquainted with nature. No yard? That's okay. You can still have herbs and tomatoes in pots on the porch or the window sill. If your city ordinances allow it, why not get some backyard chickens? There is a beauty to making meals with something that you raised or grew yourself, even if that something is just a sprig of rosemary to brighten your plate.

Eat in season whenever possible. Whether or not you have garden space, you can commit to eating in season by buying produce that is currently growing locally. Tomatoes, eggplant, and zucchini in the summer; winter squash and root veggies in the winter, for example. But don't get overwhelmed and feel as if you have to do a sudden complete overhaul of how you eat. You can take baby steps. Maybe visit your local grower's market, pick up some produce that's in season, and experiment cooking with it. There's a steep learning curve to cooking in season, so give yourself grace and time to learn. You'll get better at it every year.

Another benefit to becoming a regular at your local farmer's market is getting to know your local farmers. Maybe you can start by using local honey or eggs. Or you could join a community-supported agriculture (CSA) program to get a weekly farm share of produce. CSAs are a great way to connect your kitchen to your local farmer. Rather than picking out whatever your heart desires from the wide variety at the grocery store, you pick up a box of whatever the local farm is currently harvesting and learn to cook accordingly. It took some practice for me, but now I find the natural boundaries of eating seasonally really helpful. Remember, you don't have to change everything about how you eat all at once. By being intentional about food, you can lean into a deeper connection with what's on your plate that goes beyond consumer and thing-to-be-consumed.

While eating dinner doesn't sound like the most revolutionary action you can take to combat throwaway culture, I think setting aside time to prepare food and eat with family and friends is a powerful habit that will bear much fruit. There is something magical about spending an evening with friends, enjoying the beguiling smells of food being cooked, wine being poured, and laughter around the table.

If you have kids, get them involved with cooking. They'll be more likely to clean their plates if they helped grow and/or prepare the meal, I promise. Could you schedule a standing weekly date with friends to get together and share a meal? Take your time connecting with your loved ones around the table. Laugh and catch up while you wash and dry the dishes. Protect this time from work, TV, or cell phones that can distract you from connecting with others around the table and enjoying the bounty of the earth.

Know that it is never too late to begin new habits, to slow down, to savor, to learn, and to share. As I was discovering slow food and teaching myself to cook in my twenties, my mom was discovering it along with me in her late-fifties. She altered decades of food habits in order to learn about seasonal ingredients and slow food. Since we were living in the same town, we would pick up our CSA farm shares together as we discussed how to use up all that tricky eggplant.

Don't get caught up in all the "shoulds" or make the process overly burdensome. Prioritizing slow food doesn't mean never grabbing fast food again or opening anything that is sold in a box. It doesn't mean doing a complete 180 of your eating practices in one day (impossible!). But we can all benefit from the very simple practice of learning to pay attention to what we're eating and where it comes from, and enjoying it with other people. There is something sacred about gathering around the table, so don't rush it.

7

Holy Hospitality: Welcoming Christ in the Stranger

All guests who present themselves are to be welcomed as Christ, for he himself will say: I was a stranger and you welcomed me.

—*The Rule of St. Benedict*

The countertops were groaning under the weight of fragrant dishes. It was Thanksgiving Day on the farm. One of the sacrifices of our move was being so far away from our families that we couldn't make it home for every holiday. We were celebrating farm-style this year in one of the staff apartments up the road past the goat dairy. It was potluck Thanksgiving, and apart from the turkey and squash, the theme seemed to be carbs: homemade bread, macaroni and cheese, cornbread stuffing, and pies. But who's complaining? Not me.

As I looked around the table, I noticed that we were an unusual bunch. More tattoos and dreadlocks than your average Thanksgiving dinner gathering perhaps. Our wild kids played with our hosts' son (they were farm staff and friends from college). The farm interns from North Carolina, Wisconsin, Missouri, and various spots in Texas chatted with former staff from Georgia. Daniel was talking bees with a Liberian beekeeper who was visiting the farm for a few weeks before returning to Africa. There were Catholics and Protestants. Our skin colors were different. We had different food and cultural traditions, and we chatted about the must-have Thanksgiving recipes from our families and regions. I noticed a new face I didn't recognize.

We were just about to grab plates and start serving when two of the interns looked at their watches, grimaced, and started putting on the muddy boots they'd left at the door. "Goats!" they replied to our quizzical expressions. "We're on milking duty today, so just start without us."

Goats have to be milked, even on Thanksgiving. But we didn't obey the instructions to begin eating before milking duty was over. Instead, half of the crew trudged down the road to the dairy to help the work go faster.

"Who's the new guy?" I asked Daniel on our way to the dairy.

"Kevin?"

"Yeah. New intern?"

"Not an intern. He's actually a homeless guy who asked if he could sleep in the barn. He's been here a few days volunteering, lending a hand where he can." One of the farm's main missions is hospitality. Visitors to the farm are always invited to share lunch with everyone, and the farm tries to offer a place to anyone ready to volunteer and be part of the community.

We finished up the chores and brought a gallon of fresh warm goat's milk back to the table to accompany the assortment of pies. Then we started heaping food on our plates. My seat was next to Kevin's. I tried to make small talk, but he was pretty quiet. He was decidedly not my stereotype of a homeless man. He was well spoken and warm, although reserved. And he was . . . well, *fitting in* with our motley crew. Nobody seemed to think it was anything out of the ordinary to have him there. When the baby chicks escaped from their coop, he jumped right in to help gather them back, as if juvenile chicken rescue was something he did every day.

That meal at the farm really drove home for me the importance of hospitality. There is something powerful about opening your home and eating food with people, something that bonds you together and changes you. Across a table you are able to see people more clearly.

After a couple of weeks Kevin moved on, but before he did the farm staff tried to find out more about him, both for safety reasons and to see if they could help. Turns out his name wasn't really Kevin, and he was a former doctor who had lost his license after struggling through a family crisis. His family had reported him missing after he disappeared following a psychotic break. They didn't know where he was or whether he was still alive. The farm staff was able to get in touch with his mom to let her know that he was safe and that they could offer him a landing place for a few days. His mom wept tears of joy and relief over the phone. "I had been praying for something like this," she sobbed.

I wonder what would have happened if the farm had turned Kevin away. Would he ever have reconnected with his family? Would they ever have known what had become of him? While we can't help every single person in need, the Bible tells us to welcome the stranger in no uncertain terms.

Of course, how we undertake that obligation to hospitality should be discerned thoughtfully. It's not heartless to consider the safety of our own families, particularly our children. I'm not going to leave my children unattended with someone I don't know, for instance. I recently made the judgment call not to open my front door when I was home alone with the kids because the stranger knocking and yelling on my front porch was clearly under the influence. Maybe he was just looking for a former resident of our house or mixed up about where he was, but I was both unequipped to help this man and in a very vulnerable position without Daniel home. We can and should be wise, and always seek to protect our families, but most of the time the biggest threat to hospitality isn't safety but rather inconvenience. We don't want to or have time to go that extra mile. So we stay shut in—and we miss out on the blessing, the possibility of "unknowingly entertain[ing] angels" (Heb 13:2).

WE BELONG TO EACH OTHER

Hospitality is the opportunity to be used by God. Throwaway culture tells us that anything that inconveniences us is bad, that we have no real obligations to anyone but ourselves. The Christian virtue of hospitality takes the opposite perspective: Kevin was not a burden or a bother; we welcomed him to the table because what we have doesn't belong to us but to God.

One of my favorite quotes from Mother Teresa is this one: "If we have no peace, it is because we have forgotten that we belong to each other."[1] If we can remember this, then we will no longer view people in need as "someone else's problem," or worse, a problem that should be eliminated through abortion, euthanasia, or neglect. If we can remember this, more mothers can sleep soundly at night knowing others have made room for their children at their tables.

In a way, the Eucharist is the ultimate hospitality. We are invited into God's house, to his own table. When we have people over for dinner, they often want to know which of the dishes we served came from our garden, our chickens, or the livestock at the farm. That connection makes it more special. But at God's table we are served not merely what he has prepared or even grown for us; the food we receive is himself. It's the ultimate gift. And we are connected to other Christians in that miraculous moment—no longer separated by language, time, distance, or even death. We are one around the table.

This holy hospitality is a beautiful thing to mirror in our own homes. It is not only a gift of food and resources but also a gift of time and attention. Everyone needs a little hospitality. It might not be because they're struggling with homelessness or mental illness; it might be because they're feeling lonely, in need of encouragement. Maybe they just moved to town and showed up at your parish to Mass looking a little lost. A friend or loved one might need help getting back on their feet. The new family at church or your new coworker at the office may be in need of communal connection, simply addressed with your offer of "Would you like to come over for dinner?"

When he was about four years old, my son started inviting random people to our house. If you passed us in the grocery aisle, you probably received a dinner invitation. I would overhear him yelling from his favorite climbing tree to our neighbor with whom we shared our fence line: "My mom's making shepherd's pie tonight! Do you want to come over?" While we discouraged him from sharing our home address with complete strangers, we were pleased with the general intent. It should be normal to be hospitable.

WIPE OFF THE (STICKY) WELCOME MAT

Comedian Sebastian Maniscalco reminisces about his own childhood, when the doorbell would ring and the whole family would race to the door to see which friends had dropped by because they were "just in the neighborhood." Mom would bring out the special cake she had saved especially for company, and everyone would talk for hours. Now when the doorbell rings, everyone turns off the lights and pretends they're not home! These days friends rarely just show up at our door (especially without sending a text first), and the doorbell heralding an unexpected guest merits suspicion rather than excitement.

I grew up in a family that was eager to practice hospitality and had friends over at least once a week. Now I realize that our open door was not at all the norm; many of my peers grew up in homes for which dinner guests were a rarity. If you didn't grow up in a home that modeled hospitality, it can feel a little daunting at first. But as my mom always says, "Don't entertain; just have folks over!" Hospitality isn't about presenting a certain facade to guests or making yourself look good. It's about generous love and service.

Recently we had my daughter Lucy's godfather, Luke, a dear friend, over for dinner. It had been a crazy week. Our house's only bathroom was a disaster. Between the dirty clothes on the floor, bath toys scattered around, and toothpaste finger painted on the tiles by the toddler, it looked like a hurricane had come through. I didn't have time to clean up, gather discarded clothes into laundry baskets, or wipe down the counters and sink. I apologized immediately when Luke came over and he pulled me into a big hug and said, "Are you kidding? We're family." Being family around the table is so much more important than waiting until our house is picture-perfect so I can deceive friends into thinking our house is cleaner than it actually is. Sometimes (usually) the floors are sticky and the bathroom's messy and that's just life. By opening our messy lives to others, we offer intimacy that is much more important than a good impression. Each small act of hospitality carried out with love is what's valuable, not the cleanliness of our homes or impressiveness of our cooking skills.

Hospitality is a call to stop being insular. Life often pushes us into friend groups that are all in the same life stage and circumstances. It makes perfect sense to need relationships with people who can understand what you're going through and support you. I need mom friends I can vent to about never getting a chance to go into the bathroom *alone,* for instance. (How old do my kids have to be for me to enter *that* promised land?) But this natural need for commonality can often turn into creating your own little tribe or bubble and missing out on relationships with your brothers and sisters whose lives look very different. Even church programming can cause this by sorting everyone into "young professionals," "families," "singles," "seniors," and so forth. The truth is that we need one another—everybody.

Some of the most influential people in my life have children who are already grown. What a treat for us to invite these experienced parents to our home and soak up their wisdom. And some of my closest friends are single. It's heartbreaking to me that singles and marrieds often segregate themselves, because those of us in different seasons and circumstances can bless each other so greatly. Our home is a landing place for a few friends who are single and in their twenties or thirties. Some are figuring out their path in life. Others are longing to start their own families but haven't yet found the right person with whom to begin that journey. They know that they can text at a few minutes notice and show up to talk in our kitchen while we chop veggies for a meal; that they'll be showered with art projects made by our kids, who adore them. We are family to them, and they are family to us.

Married couples should take care not to neglect the singles in their community. Even the *Catechism* highlights that the doors of our homes and churches must remain open to all: "No one is without a family in this world: the Church is a home and family for everyone, especially those who 'labor and are heavy laden'" (*CCC*, 1658).

We need to support the single members of our communities who often feel excluded. But what I think often goes unnoticed is how much single folks offer their communities, how much married couples *need* their single friends. My wonderful mom friends have obligations and responsibilities to family life that make spending time together a challenge. Going to see a movie together takes weeks of planning. Having another family over for dinner can get in the way of bedtimes and the nightly routines that are easier when we're in our own homes. Our single friends, on the other hand, swing by and stay up late talking with us after the kids go to bed. They can join me for unwise Netflix-binging after my kids are in bed, a morning walk, or a much-needed chat at a coffee shop. Between refreshing conversations, a willingness to drop off takeout on a really bad day, or volunteering for last-minute child care, my single friends keep me afloat.

Extending yourself in this way to those in circumstances very different from yours can have rich dividends. One of my best friends had baby boys—twins!—last year. Since she already had a toddler, the pregnancy and first few months were understandably grueling. I brought a few meals and showed up a handful of times to babysit, but because of my family obligations, I couldn't offer her the support she really needed. Her single friends did. They ran by the grocery store for her after they finished work so her toddler would have milk and cereal the next morning, or they stopped by during lunch breaks to hold babies so she could put the toddler down for a nap. Their help was invaluable. And I imagine they didn't hate having a chance to hold a cute baby—or in this case, two cute babies. An online friend of mine took her first vacation in years with just her spouse—made possible by a single friend who generously stepped up to watch her kids overnight.

Wouldn't life be so much easier if we were willing to look outward and bless those in different circumstances? Make a home-cooked meal for the grad student starting a new program. Adopt a lonely senior at church to be a surrogate grandparent. We need each other.

Finding the Grace of Enough:
Tips for Practicing Hospitality

In a Pinterest world of unreasonable expectations for our homes and entertaining, the idea of real hospitality can get lost. But it's nothing to be nervous or overwhelmed about.

Remember what matters. When we worry that the meals we can provide on a limited food budget or the quality of our cooking matters more to our guests than connecting with us, we do them a disservice by assuming they will be uncharitable. If you think back to times when you were most comfortable and happy at someone's home, it's probably not because the house was immaculate and the food was perfect. It's probably because someone made you feel important, beloved, and part of the family.

Remember that authentic hospitality is always others-centered. I recently visited my friend Nell in St. Paul, Minnesota. After a horrifically early flight from Waco, I spent the day in airports. When I arrived at her house, Nell urged me to go upstairs to rest in the bedroom she'd prepared for me. There was a pitcher of ice water with a glass on a tray and everything set up for a hot bath. I felt like a guest at Downton Abbey. It was basically heaven, and I was reminded that good hospitality always keeps the guest in mind. Nell was probably ready to catch up with some girl talk, but she was thoughtful enough to consider what *I* needed. Her care and hospitality made me feel so very loved. When we stop to show someone that they matter to us, we are sharing with them the love that God has for each of his creatures, his love that considers each individual irreplaceable and worthy of great sacrifice. Hospitality is the practice of considering others first, being a listening ear, living life together, and sharing a meal.

Give yourself permission to do what you do best. Because we all have different gifts and circumstances, there's no one right way to practice hospitality other than seeking to serve others. When Daniel is cooking for guests, he wants to prepare a feast for them to enjoy. When I'm cooking for guests, I keep it simple in the kitchen or I'll be too stressed out worrying about the meal to be good company. If cooking fills you with terror and dread, it's 100 percent okay to order pizza so you can spend your energy loving your guests. You can even help make guests feel at home by including them in preparation, treating them as part of the family. Put them to work making tortillas or chopping onions and chat in the kitchen. Share the full experience of life around the table with them.

Dorothy Day reminds us, "Food for the body is not enough. There must be food for the soul."[2] Hospitality's most beautiful gift is not an offering of a meal or a place to rest your head but rather an antidote to the profound loneliness so many of us suffer. In chapter 5 we discussed the importance of centering our lives around the home. Because the home is the domestic church and the family is the school of love, by practicing hospitality you are truly inviting others into the life of the Church. You are opening the doors and offering a safe haven for those who might feel lost at sea. But the guest is not the only one who is blessed by the practice of hospitality. The host is blessed too. We need each other.

8

REBUILDING OUR
BROKEN COMMUNITIES

> Disregard for the duty to cultivate and maintain a
> proper relationship with my neighbor, for whose care
> and custody I am responsible, ruins my relationship
> with my own self, with others, with God and with
> the earth.
>
> —Pope Francis, *Laudato Si'*

It shouldn't take a car crash to meet your neighbors, but
sometimes that's exactly what brings them to your front
yard. It was couple of months after moving into the home
we purchased after Daniel completed his internship; homeschooling was done for the day. The lunch dishes were
washed, and all the kids were quiet in their rooms for "rest
time." I grabbed a cup of tea and a novel and invited our
goldendoodle, Olaf, to join me on the couch. It was one of
the coldest days of the year, so I wrapped up in the brown
alpaca wool blanket Daniel's grandmother had given us as
a wedding present.

We don't get many uncomfortably cold days in central Texas, but the cold that day was biting and wet and got right into the bones. A perfect day to stay home and read novels on the couch with a warm cuppa.

Out of the corner of my eye I saw a flash of color, then heard a crash. I turned to the window to see a small gray car and a burgundy van colliding in our intersection. The burgundy van drove into our yard and narrowly missed a huge oak tree. The gray car smashed into the fire hydrant at the corner of our yard, dislodged it, and was engulfed in a deluge of water that flowed up to our front porch.

My heart pounded in my chest as I dialed 911, put on my rain boots, and ran outside into the lake that was formerly my front yard. The driver and passenger in the gray car were struggling to get out of the vehicle and were completely drenched. The young woman driving the van spoke in rapid Spanish on her cell phone and sobbed, as did her two little boys in their car seats.

"Are you okay?" I called to her.

She managed to assure me, through her tears, that they were not hurt. She had called 911 and was trying to get through to her husband; her hands were shaking. The van was surrounded by quickly rising water, and the day was just getting colder.

I picked my way across the yard and touched her arm. "Can I bring your kids inside to have hot chocolate and watch a movie?"

She nodded and managed to get out of the mangled vehicle. A few minutes later, her husband had joined her on our front porch and her sons had calmed down a little, eating the tiny marshmallows off the top of their hot chocolates and watching *Rescue Bots* inside. My son had brought out every toy he owned to console them.

I made coffee and brought it outside to them so they might have something hot to hold while they waited for the police. The woman spoke perfect English and translated for her husband, Juan, when I asked about cream and sugar. I found out that they lived just three houses away and, like me, had been calling the city for ages about this dangerous intersection with no stop sign in either direction. "Well, I'm glad to meet some neighbors, but I'm so sorry it took a car accident to make it happen!" I said. She translated, and they chuckled.

Things got even more dramatic as, with teeth chattering in the cold, we watched police take the other driver away in handcuffs. Several warrants had been out for his arrest. When the police report was drawn up and everybody could leave, the youngest little neighbor started to cry because playtime was over. My son promised he could come back.

A few days later, Daniel was fixing a fence in our backyard. Juan walked across the street to introduce himself and to offer a rooster as a thank-you for sheltering his little sons from the cold and wet that day. Daniel thanked him but declined and explained in very poor Spanish that we were good with our little flock of hens squawking in the backyard and that they didn't owe us a thing. Juan offered help with the fence if we needed it.

We had neighbors. But it took a nearly fatal emergency to get to know them. Surely we can do better than this.

EMBRACING AUTHENTIC COMMUNITY

I love watching costume dramas. If it's a British costume drama, so much the better. Add some colorful townspeople and now you're really talking. I become fascinated as the story unfolds about the tight-knit community of people who are in each other's lives, for better or for worse. In a world of facade and first impressions, in which we can toss aside a relationship if it's not going as we'd like, the allure of a community that bears one another's quirks and flaws is irresistible.

Such forbearance is hard to come by in a throw-away culture, which prizes individualism over authentic community. Have an argument? Just delete the contact from your phone. But within small communities, this erasure isn't so easily carried out. When there's only one post office, sooner or later your world is going to collide with the person you want to avoid. You can't delete people from your lives so easily.

Living on the farm for a year with a couple dozen other people brought the joys and challenges of community living to the forefront. Although I learned many lessons from the experience, what jumps out the most is the issue of first impressions. Individualism is a world of first impressions. Meet someone and don't hit it off? You never have to see them again. But in true community, first impressions are revealed to be unimportant and often misleading. As most anyone who had college roommates can tell you, someone can be very charming but nearly impossible to live with. Or someone can be gruff and have a heart of gold and commitment to service.

My first impression of one of the "farmies" wasn't great. Let's call him Greg. I told Daniel our first week at the farm, "Greg is so condescending! And brusque! I don't like him at all." But I was dead wrong. While we have very different personalities and gifts, I came to absolutely *treasure* Greg. He worked harder than anyone else, always looking for another task with which to help out. He was endlessly kind to our oldest son (who can try the patience of a saint) by answering his constant questions, included him in projects even though his "help" wasn't always very helpful, and treated him as a grown-up. After a couple of months of getting to know this man through daily interactions, I was saying, "Greg is the *absolute best*! I can't believe I didn't love him right away! How could I have been so wrong?"

Community forces us to know others on a deeper level and gives us the opportunity to learn to love them, despite each person's inevitable quirks and annoyances. It provides opportunities to see how the variety of gifts and

personalities God gives to us all fit together and are necessary to the whole.

Unfortunately, authentic community can be hard to
find today. Americans are very big on individualism. The
prospect of staying in one place, sinking roots deep in a
community, and living a quiet life of service doesn't appeal
to many people. Community life feels like an imposition
on our personal desires. We like stories about that one guy
who "made it" and was able to leave his small town in the
dust to pursue his dreams.

So why is it, then, that *It's a Wonderful Life,* in which
George Bailey *doesn't* leave to pursue his dreams, is one of
the most popular films of all time? It tells a story we know
deep in our hearts to be true: our communities and our
service to others *matter.* The drumbeat of the throwaway
culture tells us not to be tied down to anything but our own
individual pursuits. Yet the longing to know and be known
never quite leaves us—it's something that can be satisfied
only within community.

Choosing connectedness over opportunity is anath-
ema to those who accept uncritically the consumeristic and
individualistic tenets of throwaway culture. You can see the
trend toward individualism and away from community
life in the emergence of suburbia, with its bigger houses
and privacy fences. When you have central air conditioning, who has the desire to sit on a neighbor's porch and
shoot the breeze? Why catch up on news while hanging the
laundry to dry when you can watch it on your own TV in
a well-appointed laundry room? After all, your neighbors
might end up being annoying or weird. Best to keep to
yourself where you're comfortable.

But our aversion to community hasn't served us very
well. We cart our kids around to playdates and classes
because neighborhood kids don't play together anymore.
Parents are depressed and overwhelmed because their support systems have vanished—and if you're a stay-at-home

parent you might not see another adult all day long. We're isolated and we're longing for community because we were created to be a part of the lives of others.

BEING NEIGHBORLY

During our year on the farm, we spent a lot of time reflecting on what would happen when Daniel's internship was over. Should we move back to Florida? Should we look for job opportunities elsewhere? There were so many directions we could go. But everything we were learning at the farm about community was forming our idea of what kind of place we would want to call home for the long term. As we spent time in prayer and discernment, we realized that Waco, Texas, was that place.

We also knew that we wanted to move to a neighborhood where people *lived*. We didn't want to hide out behind a backyard privacy fence in suburbia, with its manicured lawns and showcase exteriors. (We couldn't afford a house like that even if we wanted one.) So we found a house built in 1924 in the heart of the city—a little three-bedroom-one-bath with a backyard big enough for chickens and a goat, within walking distance of a Catholic parish and our favorite Mexican restaurant. If you leave the windows open, you can hear the church bells ringing. And because many of our neighbors keep chickens, we wake up to roosters crowing. It's like we never left the farm! Daniel put raised garden beds in the front yard to grow vegetables and nobody complained. There's no homeowner association telling us what we can and can't grow in our own yard. Our neighborhood is diverse. As white residents, we are in the minority.

We love our neighborhood, but we also love the greater community in the city of Waco. These days when I tell someone I live in Waco, they ask whether I know "that cute couple from *Fixer Upper* on HGTV." (I don't.) But Waco hasn't always had a reputation as squeaky clean as Chip and Joanna Gaines and their Magnolia Market.

Daniel and I went to Baylor University for our undergrad degrees during a time when people would say of
Waco, "Oh, where the Branch Davidians burned to death
and that basketball player was murdered?" And that was
even before the biker gang shoot-out of 2015 that killed
nine. So while the Gaines' Magnolia Market tourists do
make downtown traffic worse and the lines longer at my
favorite cafes, I can't entirely dismiss the idea that the *Fixer
Upper* phenomenon has improved the image of a town with
a rough history that dates back to May 1953. That was when
a catastrophic F5 tornado (believed by some to be the ven-
geance of God for a horrifying lynching in the early 1900s)
plunged the booming central Texas town into a depression. Waco never quite recovered, and moviemakers still
shoot here to make films about the '50s because, until very
recently, the streets appeared to be stuck half a century in
the past.

When I moved to Waco for college, the city was beginning to wake up. Over the past fifteen years it has moved
forward by leaps and bounds. Waco is now full of gems,
including the little cafe with farm-to-table lunch, where the
owner doesn't take a paycheck and instead pours her earn-
ings back into the Waco community. A hundred-year-old
movie theater plays old films for a couple of bucks. Waco
neighborhoods throw exciting block parties, including our
own small neighborhood's oversized Halloween extrava-
ganza with thousands of trick-or-treaters. Businesses are
generous to the large homeless population. Stunning Catholic churches offer Spanish-language Masses for Waco's
diverse residents.

It's a wonderful town, despite the fact that Waco is still
battling major problems that you won't see on *Fixer Upper*:
poverty, racial inequality, crime. It's not all pretty. But Waco
is big on *community*. Wacoans need each other, and we know
it.

Or at least we know it *now*. When Daniel and I first settled into life in our new neighborhood after living in an intentional community for a year, we discovered that we still had a lot to learn about what it means to be neighborly.

The day of my daughter Gwen's fourth birthday, we were scrambling to ready the house for guests, make a grocery run for cupcake ingredients, and roast a pig over hot coals in the backyard (the farm had a few too many piglets, so we decided to buy one and make it a Hawaiian-themed party). Daniel noticed that our neighbors had been out in the hot June sun for hours, working on a truck.

"Do you know how long they've been out there?" he asked me.

"No, I hadn't noticed."

"*Eight hours*. And see that guy, Jack? It's not even his truck. It's the other guy's truck, Francisco's."

Jack was the friendly neighbor with whom we shared a fence line. At almost two feet taller than I am, me, he towered over us with a warm smile and a gap between his front teeth, his clothes covered in grease from the truck.

"He's a mechanic," Daniel explained. "I asked him what they were doing, and he said he was just helping out 'because they're neighbors.' Francisco's English isn't great, so Jack helped him order the parts he needed. And he's been helping him fix the truck all day."

That kind of generosity blew me away. The idea of spending eight hours of my weekend helping someone with my area of expertise just because we happen to live next door sounded completely foreign to me. I would probably laugh in someone's face if they asked for eight hours of free blogging help, even if that person was my own mother. I am so steeped in a culture that sees time as money and money as the highest good—the throwaway culture that refuses to see people and God's work as the real priority. What if I could really live out what the Gospel calls us to? What if I could remember that my life and my time are not my own but God's? That it's all a gift and that if I am to imitate Christ in any way, I must learn to pour it out for others?

I looked outside again—at the black mechanic who didn't speak Spanish and the Mexican immigrant struggling with English—and saw what it really means to be neighborly: a willingness to serve generously, despite inconvenience, difference, language barriers, and Texas heat.

Daniel invited them in for roast pig, and Jack was able to stop by. Bringing a small gift for the birthday girl, he shared some pork and some cake with us. "Back to work!" he said as he headed outside to make more progress on the truck before nightfall.

Wow. We have amazing neighbors, I thought to myself.

THE COMMUNITY OF THE CHURCH

While most of you probably won't end up living in an intentional community like the farm, you probably have neighbors and can likely see their houses from your driveway. We all live in a community of some kind, even if you live out in the country. Rather than advocating for everyone to move to a small town or take on community living like we did at the farm, I think we can build community right where we are, wherever we are.

In an increasingly post-Christian world, there's a lot of buzz about creating intentional Christian community. However, a possible pitfall is forming communities that are homogenous, that just invite in those who not only share our faith but also look and live exactly like us. The Church has never been homogenous. It always pushes us out of our comfort zones into community that stretches us. I would posit that your local parish is likely the best place to invest your time if you want to promote Christian community.

When Gwen was barely two, she could not make it through Mass in the pew. When she had reached the threshold at some point during the Liturgy of the Eucharist, I would carry her to the back of the church where we would visit a statue of St. Joseph that she especially loved. She would wave and beam at the parishioners walking back to their pews after receiving the Blessed Sacrament. One Sunday she greeted an unkempt man wearing an old military coat and multiple bandanas around his head. He grinned back at her exuberant "Hi!"

I'd seen him often in the adoration chapel. He lights a lot of votives, and he prays out loud and talks to himself. He's homeless. But we both went to the adoration chapel for the same reason: to be with Jesus. Jesus is the one, and maybe only, thing we have in common.

I'm often not nearly as good as my children at interacting with people who are different from me. My instinct is to stay in my cozy circle of friends where I am comfortable. That was true before we became Catholic too. I grew up in churches that catered to young, white, middle-class families. In college, Daniel and I tried out the "undergrad" church before settling instead on the church where lots of our professors and grad student friends attended. Until our conversion to the Catholic faith, I'd never been part of a church that wasn't comprised of primarily white, middle-class attendees like myself. It's only natural to gravitate toward people who are like us: people we get along with, who like us and make sense to us; people we agree with, who make us comfortable. But if I've learned anything as a Catholic, it's that faith will force you out of your comfort zone.

The same homeless man my toddler greeted stood in line next to us waiting for the simple Lenten meal in the parish hall after Mass. A priest who often advocated for him and helped him find places to sleep waved him over for a chat. I was suddenly reminded of a quote in the news from Rob Bell, former megachurch pastor turned Oprah Winfrey Network show host, talking about why he and his wife no longer attend a church: "We have a little tribe of friends. We have a group that we are journeying with.

There's no building. We're churching all the time. It's more of a verb for us."[1]

A little tribe of friends. It makes me think of the gang of pals in the sitcom *How I Met Your Mother*—twenty-somethings who are all besties and hang out at their favorite bar, MacLaren's Pub. They eat Thanksgiving dinner together every year. They go to one another's weddings. They're with one another through thick and thin (well, for the most part). They're in the same place in life; they're all white and middle class. They all went to college. They're a little tribe of friends.

I have great friends. Their friendship is a gift from God. But hanging out with my friends as we journey through life together is a pathetic substitute for the Church. The Church is not where we chill with our besties. The Church is where we are bound together, despite our differences, because of something beyond ourselves: Christ.

What do I have in common with the homeless man in Mass? The man whose clothes are unwashed, who talks to himself and, after receiving Communion, gestures erratically as if blessing all the parishioners standing next to him? What on earth do we have in common?

What do I have in common with the old woman whose walker squeaks across the chapel floor, the African immigrant who stops to pray in the adoration chapel each morning on his way to work, the middle-aged woman who sways and whispers to herself as she attends daily Mass, the Filipino doctor, the family with ten kids, the college students who gather in the chapel and sing while Holy Saturday turns to Easter Sunday, the young couple suffering from infertility, the single guy in his forties? Perhaps nothing. We may have nothing in common except for the only thing that matters.

In Rumer Godden's brilliant novel *In This House of Brede*, the protagonist Philippa says, "One of the good things about a Catholic church is that it isn't respectable.

You can find anyone in it, from duchesses to whores, from tramps to kings."[2] Yes. Here we all are. Sinners. All drawn together in one flesh because only in the Church can we partake of Jesus' Body and Blood. Only in the Church can we receive this grace. Although we might never have chosen to sit together at a pub, the Church reminds us that we are brothers and sisters, family. The Eucharist is what binds us together.

The Church is not a little tribe of people like me. It is the immigrant, the lawyer, the blue-collar worker, the single mom. It's filled with people with whom I have nothing in common. Some of whom I don't even like and some who probably don't like me. We are not comfortable together. But we are one; not broken up according to ethnicity, socio-economic status, education, and certainly not by cliques. From its inception, the Church was revolutionary for this very reason: its unity. Slave, free, Jew, Gentile, rich, poor, meeting together in the catacombs, all eating from the same table of grace over the blood of the martyrs.

We are offered the chance to nurture that community beyond the walls of the parish and to offer love and connection to those all around us, whether it's someone sitting in the pew behind us or our next-door neighbor. But we have to step away from the busyness of life to have the margins to do so.

Finding the Grace of Enough: Tips for Rebuilding Community

The Bible instructs us to show hospitality to strangers—but what can we do when *we* are the ones who are starting over or feeling isolated? We all long for connection, but committing to other people isn't painless. Being in community can be highly frustrating, requiring sacrifice (just like everything worth doing: marriage, getting a degree, raising kids, becoming more holy, perfecting a macaron recipe). So how do we go about it?

Get to know your neighbors. Make some cookies, go over to their homes, and knock on their doors. You don't have to wait for them to have a terrifying car crash in your front yard. Introduce yourself; maybe get a phone number so you can text if there's an issue in the neighborhood or you want to invite them over for dinner. Depending on where you live, your neighbors might all be a lot like you or they might be very different. We often handpick our circle of friends from people who are just like us—mine is often full of people who like chatting about twentieth-century British novels and making farm-to-table meals. But when you make an effort to talk to someone God has dropped into your life, you find that you do have things in common despite different life circumstances, tastes, and beliefs. Getting to know your neighbors is a great way to step out of the echo chambers we create for ourselves and understand real people.

Make your presence known at church. Reach out and have your priest over for dinner. Start volunteering at your parish. Stay for coffee or breakfast after Mass and meet someone new. Start going to daily Mass. Join (or start) an adult education class or reading group.

Get involved in your community. There are plenty of ways to do this, and often not enough people willing to take on the work. (My husband discovered this when he showed up to his first community meeting and came home a little shell-shocked having been voted in as president of the neighborhood association.) Step outside your front door and see who God has placed in your community. Teach a workshop at your local library. Have a block party. Help out your neighbors. Your actions will be contagious.

9

THE INTERNET:
ISOLATOR OR COMMUNITY BUILDER?

> Emails, text messages, social networks, and chats can also be fully human forms of communication. It is not technology which determines whether or not communication is authentic, but rather the human heart and our capacity to use wisely the means at our disposal.
> —Pope Francis

"*Who* are we staying with tonight?" the kids asked us from the back seat of our minivan.

"The Tighes."

"Do they have kids?"

"Yup. You'll have new friends to play with."

"Have we met the Tighes before?"

"Nope."

"How did you and Daddy meet them?"

"Well . . . we haven't yet. We know them from . . . the internet."

Daniel and I burst out laughing. What were we *thinking*? Taking our family to the home of people we only knew

from Twitter was weird. Were we at the beginning of a hor-
ror film plot? Would we survive the night?

Karen Tighe's thoughts were along the same lines when
her husband, Tommy, told her that his Twitter friends were
going to be in the Bay Area and he'd invited them to stay.
What had he signed her up for? They could be lunatics!

I think she was pleasantly surprised when we arrived,
stinky from a few days of camping but not looking very
serial killer-ish. For a couple of days we shared meals, said
bedtime prayers together, and stayed up late after our kids
fell asleep to talk about natural family planning and social
media. No one got murdered, and we're still friends.

It was 2015, and we were on a road trip just before
our move to the farm in Texas, and the Tighes weren't the
only friends we connected with whom we had only known
from the ol' World Wide Web. We'd also had dinner with
a blogging friend and her family in Louisville, spent a day
with online friends in Boise, stayed four days with a family
in Los Angeles that we had previously only emailed with,
and slept in a renovated school bus in Oregon owned by
another internet buddy. But perhaps the most beautiful
experience of internet connection turned real life was going
to the Abbey of Gethsemane in Kentucky. A Twitter friend
coordinated things so we could have dinner with his family,
the prior, and one of the brothers at the hermitage where
monk and writer Thomas Merton had lived.

On that sticky summer night, the grown-ups sat on
the porch of Merton's hermitage sharing favorite poems
while the children ran around with pizza slices. The monks,
used to the silence of monastic life, were chuckling at the
kids' questions, antics, and noise. It was a beautiful evening
juxtaposing the vocation to religious life and the vocation
to marriage as each ministered to the other until the bells
chimed for Compline and the two monks jumped into an
ATV to make it back to the abbey in time for prayer. (We got
a great photo of that, don't worry.) While I'm pretty sure

that Thomas Merton would have hated how social media can distract from the spiritual life with its endless mental noise, I think he would have enjoyed that evening at his hermitage, compliments of Twitter.

UN-SOCIAL MEDIA

Unfortunately our use of technology doesn't always lead us to delightful evenings with monks. Instead, our culture's oversaturation of virtual life can certainly result in distraction from prayer and the reflection necessary for spiritual growth as well as isolation from relationships and real-life interactions. A perfect example of this technological isolation is the Bodega startup designed to supply pantry boxes of nonperishables in apartment buildings. Instead of walking a few steps down the sidewalk to a corner store and purchasing from the person behind the counter, you can use an app on your phone to buy what you need. You don't have to step out of your own building, and there's no human interaction required.

It's easy to see how the way we use technology for extreme convenience can contribute to isolation, but the rise of the internet is not the primary source of our modern disconnectedness. We discussed in chapter 5 how modern families are becoming isolated from one another and how we desperately need to revive a home-centered life that can bring families back together and value the gift of the home. In chapter 8, we discussed how our communities are disconnected and outlined ways we can improve that pervasive problem. *Neither* of these issues are attributable to the internet. These troubles began long ago, when our grandparents' or great-grandparents' generation left tight-knit communities to seek new opportunities in a more mobile society.

While it is still possible to find extended families living within the same communities for generations, that is certainly no longer the norm. The same pursuit of opportunity that prompted families to move from their farms to the cities, in time prompted families to move away from the cities to the space and privacy of the suburbs. Urban neighborhoods declined, and urban parishes emptied. In the suburbs, society became isolated and fragmented, leaving a deep thirst for community. All these things happened well before anyone had heard of the internet.

Ironically, it is this *longing for connection* that has caused recent generations to turn to technology as a remedy for isolation. But virtual life is a poor substitute for authentic connection. Obsessive social media use and need for constant virtual affirmation harm us rather than help reconnect us. We want to reach out, but we can easily end up focusing back in on ourselves instead.

My freshman year of college, Facebook was born. My transition to adulthood has gone hand in hand with the rise of social media. Now as a work-from-home mom with online writing and podcasting as my occupation, I understand better than ever that the internet never sleeps. While it's easy to understand overconsumption of food, resources, clothes, and other tangible things, one might forget that throwaway culture's consumption obsession can also extend to media. It is a constant siren song of activity and content to be consumed, often just an arm's reach away. While the evils of pornography and other online dangers are obvious, what Pope Francis calls "mental pollution" can be equally destructive (*LS* 47). As I scroll through Twitter, snippets of news and information give me a highly superficial understanding of events and ideas. But they fail to offer me real comprehension on a deep level of anything at all.

In *Laudato Si'*, the Holy Father writes that "true wisdom, as the fruit of self-examination, dialogue and generous encounter between persons, is not acquired by a mere accumulation of data which eventually leads to overload and confusion" (*LS* 47). I think one of the most dangerous results of our overconsumption of media is the false sense of knowing. We can convince ourselves that we are informed about many things but fail to truly know anything in depth. We fail to become wise in our attempt to retweet the latest news and conversations and miss out on true encounter with ideas and people. I have yet to meet anyone active on social media who has not experienced that sense of "overload" that keeps one from clear thinking and engaged living.

We run a real risk of burying what's truly important in an avalanche of mental clutter. Pope Francis claims that "when media and the digital world become omnipresent, their influence can stop people from learning how to live wisely, to think deeply and to love generously. In this context, the great sages of the past run the risk of going unheard amid the noise and distractions of an information overload" (*LS* 47). The concern is not merely the mental overwhelm and superficiality of what is consumed online but also what we lose when we fill our time with this kind of consumption.

Instead of nourishing our souls with prayer, spiritual reading, and real human connection, we can starve in the constant barrage of quick media. We can use technology as a temporary distraction from our spiritual poverty. Neither the flood of information nor the superficial affirmation we may receive from our use of technology can fulfill our deepest desires for intimacy with God, our human desire for connection with other people, or our intellectual quest for what is true and good.

THE QUEST FOR AUTHENTIC FRIENDSHIP

This consumerist attitude toward the internet warps our attitude toward relationships. Human interactions can be both highly rewarding and challenging. Replacing real relationships with online communications fails to satisfy us for long; we crave real human connection on a deep level, though the connection can be messy and awkward at times. What is more, social media can quickly erode some important social skills, including conflict resolution and meaningful personal connection. My single friends tell me that the rise of apps such as Tinder are actually making it *more difficult* rather than less to meet people; having become accustomed to swiping through people on a screen, singles are less likely to strike up a conversation in real life.

Pope Francis warns that turning from deep human relationships to virtual interactions can lead to merely "contrived emotion" and can "shield us from direct contact with the pain, the fears and the joys of others and the complexity of their personal experiences" (*LS* 47). We might experience the immediate gratification of "likes" but miss out on the depth of genuine human relationships, the good *and* the painful aspects.

The superficiality of online relationships can be a result of the lack of sacrifice and effort it takes to communicate. Virtual friendships can suffer from the same superficiality of coworker friendships. You might be "friends" with a coworker whom you see every day because of being in the same location. It takes no extra effort to spend time with her, and you already have a topic to talk about (work). But the lack of intentionality it takes to maintain the friendship often results in it quickly dissipating when you no longer work together.

When we "show up" to social media and communicate with online friends because they pop up in our feeds, we are not truly making any kind of effort or sacrifice to do the work of what a real friendship requires. It's easy to like an Instagram picture of someone's cute baby or wish someone happy birthday on their Facebook timeline. It takes actual effort to offer to babysit or show up with a birthday cake. We can even become stretched so thin maintaining hundreds of superficial relationships that we lack the time we would need to invest in authentic friendships.

The distance between people as we use our screens rather than face-to-face discussions to interact can serve as a barrier protecting us from the joy and suffering of real intimacy. It protects us from vulnerable love. In his book *The Four Loves*, C. S. Lewis writes, "Love anything and your heart will be wrung and possibly broken. If you want to make sure of keeping it intact you must give it to no one, not even an animal. Wrap it carefully round with hobbies and little luxuries; avoid all entanglements. Lock it up safe in the casket or coffin of your selfishness. But in that casket, safe, dark, motionless, airless, it will change. It will not be broken; it will become unbreakable, impenetrable, irredeemable. To love is to be vulnerable."[1]

Real intimacy requires vulnerability (we will explore a different aspect of this vulnerability in the next chapter, which is about authentic intimacy within marriage). By hiding behind our screens, we can end up dissatisfied with our relationships and very lonely in our voluntary isolation, and even slaves to a serious technology addiction. Those of us with laptops or smartphones must ask ourselves: Is our use of technology drawing us away from real happiness? Are we failing to live wisely, think deeply, and love generously because of the mental pollution of digital life? Are we avoiding prayer and the practices that set us free and in right relationship with God? Are we neglecting authentic human connection for the easy but ultimately unsatisfying virtual affirmation of social media?

MAKING TECHNOLOGY WORK FOR YOU

Aside from all the possible negative consequences of technology, I believe that technology can also positively influence our lives and build true community.

Technology is a tool. Like any tool, we must learn to use it correctly, to help us build community rather than distract and disconnect us.

A healthy use of technology *can* be a path to a more deeply connected community. While we can't change the layout of cities, the breakup of families, or the disconnection of communities overnight, we can harness technology creatively and wisely to nurture our relationships and spiritual lives. As a blogger, much of my work is done on the internet, and I've seen how it can be a tool of connection and a tool for evangelization.

Obviously if we "know" people all over the world through our phones and computers but don't know our next-door neighbor's name, we're taking the easy way out. But connectedness in our real-life relationships and digital life doesn't have to be an either/or. I think we can reach out in our communities *and* use the internet in a healthy way to offer support and share the truth of the Gospel. This is possible when we use technology as a bridge from our highly isolated modern society to the sort of real community that we've been missing for generations.

The internet can be godsend to those who are incredibly isolated and can't see a clear path to authentic community. It can be a blessed stepping-stone that leads to genuine friendships and support. When I was a stay-at-home mom of three kids under the age of five, there were days when I felt incredibly lonely and isolated. Social media offered me not just virtual emotional support by connecting me with other like-minded moms in similar circumstances but also helped me nurture and maintain real-life friendships that were difficult to invest in face-to-face at the time. There were many sleep-deprived days when packing up a strong-willed four-year-old, a needy two-year-old, a nursing newborn, and the accompanying diaper bag, snacks, and water bottles in the car for a playdate was simply more than I could handle. Texting with local friends who were home with sick toddlers or similarly too overwhelmed to venture beyond home was a lifeline.

Of course, in an age when everyone lived with or at least near extended family, and when neighbors would hang up laundry together and talk, the kind of isolation many young parents experience would have been highly unusual. But since we don't live in that world anymore, we need a way to rebuild that kind of community and technology can help us do just that. While a Facebook message from a fellow mom isn't the same as a friend showing up to help you care for children and keep you company, it is a step in the right direction to a more connected life.

Many of my virtual friendships have blossomed into authentic and important relationships, far beyond the superficial. An online group of ten fellow moms and Catholic bloggers that was born five years ago has been an invaluable support to me during difficult times. Walking with each other through big moves, unexpected pregnancies, infertility, miscarriage, medical crises, and other struggles has born the fruit of authentic friendship. Most of us have met in real life, despite needing to travel long distances to make it happen. The beauty of these friendships shows me that building community through technology is possible and simply requires effort and intentionality.

This ability to connect beyond our physical locations has also benefitted many families by providing the opportunity to work remotely. Our family life is more home-centered due to the flexibility of my work-from-home situation, a setup that was rare before the rise of the internet. While still contributing to our family income, my work can fit around our home life instead of the other way around.

Technology can be a great tool even *within* our real-life communities. One of my favorite ideas for promoting neighborliness and combating the throwaway culture (as well as harnessing the internet for good) is the Buy Nothing Project. It's a hyperlocal gift economy that has chapters all over. A friend of mine founded a chapter for our part of town, and it works like this: If you have something you're not using, you can post it on the Buy Nothing group's Facebook page. It might be clothes your children have outgrown, books you don't plan to read again, extra paper plates from a birthday party, or an unused chair. No one pays you for your items or barters for them. They are gifts. You meet up with an actual real live person who wants or needs that item.

I love this project because it keeps us from tossing items that could be used and needed by another family. I once heard a story about Pope Francis, before he became pope, collecting the rubber bands from his daily newspaper and giving them back to his postman so they could be reused. What attention to detail! Instead of being trapped in a house of clutter, paying for storage, or filling up your attic, you can ensure that those unneeded items in your home can be used by someone who wants and needs them—by your very own neighbors. By participating in a gift economy, you are part of a system that is not constantly focused on the monetary value of things. And you can meet your neighbors to boot. Several pieces of furniture in our house are from our neighbors. Other families' kids are wearing my youngest child's hand-me-downs. It's a beautiful thing. Buy Nothing groups are a perfect example of how with a little creativity, we can use technology to strengthen our communities rather than isolate ourselves.

Because of the obvious pitfalls of virtual life, it's easy to be down on technology and to dismiss the possibility of authentic good emerging from the internet. But the fruits of online connections can be beautiful. A year after we showed up on their doorstep, the Tighes' son Luke died just after his birth. Halfway through the pregnancy, they had learned of a tragic medical condition that would take their son from them as soon as he entered the world. The world of Catholic Twitter covered them with prayer and support. Their vulnerability in sharing about this tragedy in the light of their faith helped other grieving families find solace by communicating with a couple who could understand their loss.

The story of Luke's young life and his parents' faithfulness and care for him in a pregnancy they knew would end in loss impacted and inspired thousands. The possibilities for prayer and evangelization that technology offers are huge.

Finding the Grace of Enough:
Tips for Building Your Village (at Home and Far Away)

In the interest of full disclosure, not letting my phone take over my life is a struggle for me. It is a difficult balancing act. But there are practical steps we can take to using technology in a healthy way.

Put intentional space between you and your phone. Plug it in to charge in a bedroom and leave it there instead of within arm's reach. Walk away from your phone to read a real book, have a cup of tea, or go outside. Try to break out of the routine of looking at a screen constantly out of habit.

Take up intentional spiritual practices that have nothing to do with a screen. Get a print book or devotional for your prayers instead of using an app. I may begin the day with the best of intentions to pray, but if I pick up my phone to open my Liturgy of the Hours app I may get distracted and end up checking all my social media channels and wasting twenty minutes, using up the time I had set aside to pray.

Remove any distracting apps. At the very least, turn off notifications to quiet the siren song that wants to draw you back to your phone. The less frequently you are tempted to unlock your phone, the less time you'll spend on it.

Curate carefully whom you follow. If following a certain person is a near occasion of sin (triggers envy or wrath), don't hesitate to remove that temptation by unfollowing. I have never regretted stepping back from someone's online persona or any parts of digital life that are causing problems for me.

Be honest with yourself about your technology use. What are your motivations for using technology? Are you sharing photographs on social media because it brings joy to your parents to see photos of their grandchildren, or are you sharing photographs on social media because the likes give you a false sense of value or popularity?

While embracing technology holds the possible dangers of mental pollution, narcissism, isolation from real-life relationships, and distraction from the inner quiet that precipitates prayer, it *can* be used to support the isolated, build a bridge to better communities, improve family life, and even spread the Gospel. The internet isn't going anywhere, so we have to harness it with intention to draw us into better relationships with God and each other.

PART III

CENTERING OUR

DISCONNECTED

LIVES AT HOME

10

Generous Love: Discovering Authentic Intimacy

Let us remember that love lives through sacrifice and is nourished by giving. Without sacrifice, there is no love.

—St. Maximilian Kolbe

It was early March, and the sun was shining on the wooden platform next to the farm's Education Building, where we often sat to eat lunch on fair-weather days. While the kids climbed a nearby mulberry tree, some of us were soaking up the rays and enjoying the retreat of winter before afternoon work began for farmies and the naptime battle began for me.

"I know you've got your hands full now, but do you want more kids someday?" one of the interns asked.

"Yeah, we do. In fact, if I didn't have such difficult pregnancies, we'd probably have several more than we have already."

"Wow! How many do you want?"

"Honestly, I don't have a number in mind," I laughed. "We joke about wanting enough for a Quidditch team, but you never know. We're Catholic, so . . . it's important to us to be open to life."

"So . . . don't answer if it's too personal, but what exactly does that mean? Do you really not use birth control, like . . . at all?"

"It's fine. I don't mind talking about it. Yes, that's right. As Catholics we believe that a healthy reproductive system doesn't need medical intervention. We believe that sex belongs in marriage and that giving ourselves entirely to each other includes our fertility. We believe that children are a gift. It's actually really simple, but it took a while for the pieces to fit together for us. So we don't use birth control—at least, we don't use it anymore. . . ."

Our attitude toward children and fertility has shifted a lot since we were first married, but I can remember those early days vividly.

It was 2008 and I was running late to my 8:00 a.m. class. Daniel and I had been married for a year, and I should have been stuffing books in my backpack and biking to campus. Instead I was vomiting in our bathroom. I hadn't eaten a big enough breakfast to counteract the nausea that arrived every morning when I popped my birth control pill. So, yet again, I was throwing up. And I was *over it*.

It wasn't just the nausea. It was headaches too. Even worse, the mood swings. I was an emotional basket case most of the time. Crying at the drop of a hat, fuming over nonexistent slights, and feeling despair over . . . who knows what. It took several months (and a pretty serious toll on our young marriage) to connect the dots: the Pill was making me sick.

Growing up in a middle-class Protestant bubble, I had never questioned that I would be on birth control. I'd take the Pill until we were financially secure with established careers and 100 percent ready to become parents. (In reality, no one is ever 100 percent ready to become a parent—but it took us some time to realize that.) It hadn't occurred to me that there was another option, another way of doing things and approaching the question of our fertility.

Somewhere in the back of my mind I'd heard that Catholics were against birth control. *But surely that was just back in olden times,* I told myself. *Nobody actually rejected contraception in this day and age, right? You'd have to be crazy!*

But as I faced the side effects of the contraceptive model I had chosen, and it dawned on me what a toll it was taking on me to alter my body chemistry just to avoid pregnancy, I began to wonder if I was actually the crazy one.

It was around this time that I was starting to feel a serious pull toward Catholicism. I had been introduced to the writings of the Church Fathers in some of my college classes and became interested in the rich theology of the faith. I started reading everything I could get my hands on about Catholic doctrine. Instead of immediately dismissing it, as I had in the past, I was ready to entertain the idea that the Church could be right about some things. I began to think that one of those things was its teachings on sexuality. Was what the Church taught about the theology of the body an explanation for my unease with the whole idea of contraception?

What if sex was designed to be unitive and procreative? I wondered. *What if removing my fertility from the equation wasn't achieving what I always thought it was supposed to for newlyweds: a strong marriage, happiness, and no inconvenience? What if accepting a contraceptive mind-set wasn't making us happier at all and was, in fact, making me sick and depressed?* As I popped those pills and waited for the wave of nausea to hit me like a ton of bricks, I started to squirm a little bit. What was I doing to myself? Did it even make any sense?

"I can't do this!" I sobbed to Daniel after a morning of nausea and an afternoon of emotional meltdowns. "I don't want to feel like this anymore. I want to feel like *myself*."

Having watched me transform from the generally reasonable human being he had proposed to into the emotional wrecking ball he'd been married to for several months, he fully supported this motion. "What should we do instead?" he asked.

"I don't know, but I'm not refilling my prescription. I am *done*."

After that conversation with Daniel, I never got another refill. We decided we would look into natural family planning (NFP) and start charting my cycle to postpone pregnancy because we didn't consider ourselves at all ready to become parents.

Of course, life was a whirlwind of final thesis edits, job applications, and graduation events. *I'll read about NFP in a couple of months. After graduation,* I told myself. *I think I have the general idea.* (Spoiler alert: I didn't have the general idea. I'm sure you'll be shocked to discover that the five minutes I spent googling NFP did not equip me with a thorough understanding of the complexities of my fertility symptoms.)

You see where this is going, right?

Graduation came and went. We celebrated our second anniversary with a trip to Disney World. My NFP research date was on the calendar for when we returned home. We dreamed and discussed the future while waiting in line in the hot Florida sun for the next roller coaster.

"What do you think about starting a family in like . . . five or six years?" I dreamily asked Daniel. Yes. That would be wise and prudent. I could imagine us having a baby in five years. We would surely have life figured out by then. We would be homeowners, and I'd turn into the sort of person who gets manicures and has a day planner. Future Responsible Me might wear blouses instead of T-shirts of my favorite bands. We would be ready then.

As I prepared to begin my first big-girl job postgraduation, I felt a little . . . off, but I was in complete denial as to why. A close friend noticed that I was napping frequently, snacking constantly, and crying at unreasonable moments (such as when I opened the fridge only to discover we'd run out of sour cream—true story). She told me to hop in the car so we could pick up a pregnancy test.

"Oh, please. I'm *so* not pregnant. I'm about to learn that NFP thing, and I'm only twenty-two. Can we stop at Chick-fil-A on the way, though? Because I'm *starving*."

"You are unbelievable. Just get in the car," she ordered.

"So is that a yes or a no as to chicken biscuits for second breakfast?"

It was a yes (she must have remembered the sour cream meltdown), and then we were on our way to purchase my first pregnancy test: the "two lines if you're pregnant, one line if you're not" kind. When we got home it was . . . inconclusive. At least to a woman in denial like myself. Was that a second line? Surely not. It's barely there! But after asking my friend to be the control group (and her test looked undeniably different), I was willing to consider the possibility. We went back to the store for the digital test that will abrasively blink "PREGNANT" if it's positive, as if you've just set off a gestation alarm.

The strangest thing happened to me while I waited for the results of that test. My fears and anxieties about an unplanned pregnancy were swallowed up by a deep and undeniable desire for this baby. As the bossy pregnancy test blinked the news that I was a mother, I experienced an overwhelming knock-me-to-my-knees gratitude. The memory of that gut-punched-with-love feeling brings tears to my eyes to this day. I didn't even know I wanted to be pregnant—in fact, I would have argued the opposite seconds prior—but the love I felt for my baby washed away everything but a desperate prayer of thanks to God. "I know I don't deserve this baby. I don't really know what's going to happen next, God. But I am so grateful."

By dropping the Pill and refusing to treat fertility as a disease to be medicated, we were led to the adventure of a lifetime. For years I bought into the idea that the Pill was going to be a source of freedom for me and for women everywhere, but I was wrong. In reality, the Pill has been making lots of women sick and depressed, sometimes even causing serious medical conditions (such as blood clotting) that can be deadly.

Despite this, in many circles having a conversation about the dangers of contraception is taboo. "Question the Pill and you're questioning women's rights," we're told. Yet questioning these things is exactly what I found myself doing . . . and, in questioning, came to experience the freedom of embracing the idea that "a person's rightful due is to be treated as an object of love, not as an object for use," as St. John Paul II puts it in *Love and Responsibility*.[1]

FERTILE BLESSINGS

While eschewing contraception is still a countercultural move, millennials are more open than previous generations to the idea that treating a healthy reproductive system as broken and in need of pharmaceutical drugs might not be the best idea. Concepts such as NFP (sometimes referred to as fertility awareness method, or FAM)[2] seem to be going mainstream. The idea gaining traction is that maybe, *just maybe*, fighting the way our bodies naturally work isn't serving us well—even outside Christian circles and in secular magazines such as *Cosmopolitan*. New apps and technology that make it easier to track fertility signs are being produced all the time.

Increasing skepticism of pharmaceutical companies and a desire for more education and awareness of how our bodies are designed can also be seen in the natural birth movement. Women want to be empowered with real knowledge about their bodies instead of altering the natural systems in place.

It makes sense, of course, that the impulse to pursue a healthier lifestyle—and to ask basic questions such as "What foods were we designed to consume?" and "How were we meant to be connected to other people?"—would also cause us to wonder why we prescribe drugs for a healthy reproductive system. While secular movements are cottoning on to the idea that there may be better alternatives to the pharmaceuticals currently being used to "manage fertility," the Church reveals the goodness of God's plan for marriage and family. It explains why severing the natural connections between weighty human experiences such as sex, marriage, and fertility can cause harm and cause us to lose our grasp on abundant life.

My journey toward generous love—the self-sacrificial love that accompanies motherhood—began with a 180-degree turn from throwaway culture, which in the arena of sexuality elevates pleasure and convenience above every other consideration. As I came to see the emptiness and selfishness of this, and the beauty of the Church's vision for marriage, I found myself examining lifelong assumptions about love, and I began to recognize for the first time my failure to love in other relationships.

Had I ever before loved a person for their own sake, just because they existed, instead of for what they could do for me? I wasn't sure, but I was doubtful. Even my love for Daniel was driven by a consumptive mind-set—I had loved him for what he brought to my life, because he made me happy.

But when I became a mother, the generous love placed in my heart for my baby began spilling into my other relationships. As God wove my first child together in my womb, a new work had begun in my heart. Yet it was not an easy road. Learning to live out sacrificial love was a brutal journey for me. I had been entrenched so long in my own selfishness that, at first, parenthood was often an agonizing experience of God battering my heart so it could become more like his. But slowly and excruciatingly through months of extreme morning sickness during pregnancy and months of sleep deprivation with a newborn, layer after layer of stone was chipped away to reveal a flesh-and-blood heart that was finally learning how to love.

LOVE THAT CONQUERS

At a retreat I attended recently, a priest said that choosing to become parents in the modern world is absolute lunacy. Our world is broken, secularism is rampant, and there is just so much that could go wrong. But, he reminded us, it's an act of extraordinary courage, the kind of foolish hope that the Gospel is built on—the story that seemed impossible, love beating death; a story we can participate in but cannot control.

As a new Catholic, I discovered that eschewing birth control and being open to life had planted us in merely the first circumstance in a chain of situations in which we were faced with the reality that we are never really in total control of our lives. When our firstborn tumbled into the world, I thought if I did everything a certain way, I would get a certain kind of child. If I figured out the right bedtime routine, he would finally start sleeping longer than an hour at a time. If I had consistent discipline, he would never misbehave. What resulted was a rude awakening, literally—frustrating nights and sleep-deprived days with a hopelessly colicky baby who never slept and screamed in misery when he was awake. We were reminded again a bit later, driven to despair at the sheer force of will of a spirited toddler with . . . ahem . . . leadership potential. It took me a long time to understand that I was not in control of this new little soul. I was there to love, teach, and guide, but that's where my influence ended.

We want to control our lives. We want to set out with a plan and watch it unfold as we desire. Our attempt to control our fertility is a piece of that. Avoiding parenthood or wanting to call it quits so we can "move on with our real lives" is born from this desire to control. But that's a false security; it's not how the world works. Despite what we tell ourselves, we are simply not in control. Hurricanes wipe out communities despite our emergency plans and efforts to protect them. Illness can destroy our best-laid plans. And we all know couples who were surprised by a pregnancy despite whatever method of contraception they were using. Life is an adventure orchestrated by God, and our attempts to be in the driver's seat will always result in mere frustration. Why? Because this is not the way of authentic love, which involves the total surrender of self.

Authentic love calls for sacrifice. That is true of all of us. Whether it's being up with a baby all night, caring for an aging parent, giving a hurting friend a landing place in your home for a while, or becoming a foster parent, we will be called on to sacrifice. That is the way of the Cross, and we are not offered anything else. It's easy to think of parenthood as a season of sacrifice that ends so we can move on with our lives. But neither Christ nor the saints ever model living for ourselves. God never tells us, "Wow, thanks for your service. You've done your time and please enjoy the next four decades of your life living just for yourself. You've been serving others for awhile so grab your sunscreen and enjoy your remaining years drinking cocktails in Aruba." Can you imagine that being the final chapter of a saint's life? We are called to live out generous love in whatever opportunities present themselves to us.

The contraceptive mind-set (that removes fertility from its connection to sexuality) and its tragic sister, abortion, are facets of throwaway culture intended to eliminate the need to embrace this call to sacrificial love. Yet this is a journey we need to take, no matter what our vocation might be. Whether we're called to married life or religious life, and whether or not there are children in our future, we are all called to lives of generous outpouring for others. In our lives, God used parenthood to help us begin this journey, but it is not the only path to learning Christlike love.

For us, the Church's teachings on marriage and fertility made sense and drew us like a magnet into the arms of the Church. While the journey wasn't and isn't easy, we found it to be so full of joy that we wanted to experience the fullness of the truth we were discovering. In fact, that one decision to throw out my birth control pills actually led to our conversion. Our son's birth was a deep grace in our lives. While we had been toying with the idea of becoming Catholics for months, maybe even years, when we held his tiny, beautiful body for the first time, a new undeniable motivation tugged us Rome-ward.

Looking at the miracle of life, it was inconceivable to think that he wouldn't have been in our arms at all without the influence of the Church's teachings. We wanted to give this child entrusted to us the rich tradition of the Church and the grace of the sacraments. We wanted him to be washed in the waters of Baptism and received into the Church. After preparing for months through the Rite of Christian Initiation of Adults (RCIA), one beautiful night in a candlelit sanctuary we declared that we truly believed and professed the teachings of the Church. We received the precious Body and Blood of the Lord for the first time and left smelling of holy oil. We came home feeling the generous love of God in a way we never had before—the physical reminder of God's incomprehensible love asleep in our arms—not knowing that he had transformed our lives forever and pushed us right into an ocean of grace.

Finding the Grace of Enough: Tips to Living Authentic Love

While married folks are called to openness to life (and no, this doesn't mean you have to have as many children as humanly possible), how can others practice generous love? It's clear that folks called to religious life are living out sacrifice for others through their work in the priesthood or their order. But what about the single folks discerning what's ahead or even couples struggling from infertility whose empty arms may be a great sorrow to them?

Listen for God's call to generous love, but know that not all of us will experience this call through biological parenthood. God calls some to spiritual motherhood or fatherhood. Can you mentor someone in need of the wisdom and attention you could offer? Do you know someone whose parents have been unable to offer the guidance and love that is longed for? Could you make yourself available to be a special person in the life of a child with special physical or emotional needs, to support and encourage them?

Remember that, in your community, there are many vulnerable people not receiving the care they deserve as human beings created in the image of God. How can you pour yourself out for them? Can you serve the homeless or the forgotten elderly in your community?

Perhaps you haven't been called to marriage or your childrearing days are over, but your contribution to the family of God is still valuable and needed.

For engaged and married couples, research the beauty of Catholic teaching on matters of marriage, sexuality, and family life. Are you willing to consider openness to life and authentic intimacy? I'm including some resources for learning more about alternatives to contraception in the back of the book.

The possibilities for offering generous love are truly endless because there are infinite ways we can love others authentically. The opportunities we encounter will vary according to our vocations and situations in life. There is no extensive checklist to complete, just a fresh start each day to choose love and sacrifice.

11

LIVING THE GOSPEL, MOLLY WEASLEY-STYLE

> My father told me all the Weasleys have red hair,
> freckles, and more children than they can afford.
> —Draco Malfoy
> in *Harry Potter and the Sorcerer's Stone*

"Mama?"

"Yes, Bud?"

"When I grow up, I want to be rich and buy all the LEGO sets ever made!"

My heart sank. We'd been so intentional, so committed to forming our family with a focus on faith, relationships, and things that last. We lived without flushing toilets for a year, for crying out loud! And here my firstborn son was sharing his dearest ambition to have a boatload of money so he can buy all the things he wants.

He came by it honestly, I suppose. I remember being enamored with wealth as a child. There was a girl in my elementary school class with trendy clothes who lived in a veritable mansion. I remember being jealous of her huge house and what appeared to be a very glamorous life.

130

Later I discovered that her home life was very unhappy; I would have been a fool to trade my loving home for hers. But like most children, I lacked the discernment to see clearly beyond the superficial and was easily impressed by affluence.

There's no denying that "living simply" becomes more difficult and complicated after children enter the picture. It's hard to ignore all the marketing and social pressure urging us to offer our children all that they might desire. It's not easy to ignore our children's demands when they're affected by the brainwashing of commercialism. Yet all the reasons that an anticonsumerist Gospel life is beneficial for *us* still applies to our kids. When I need a shot in the arm, I draw inspiration from some of my favorite fictional characters: the Weasleys.

BECOMING MOLLY WEASLEY

Ask any *Harry Potter* fan which magical family she'd want to be born into and you'll get one answer: the Weasleys, of course! The Weasleys have a modest home, the Burrow. It's nothing fancy, in fact it's not even structurally sound, as it looks like magic is all that's holding it together. And it's full to bursting with, according to naysayers, "more children than they can afford" (seven).

The Weasleys live on one income. For them, it's secondhand clothes, used schoolbooks, bagged lunches. The paterfamilias, Arthur, isn't ambitious for worldly success but works a job he loves to support his family. Their vault at Gringotts, the wizard bank, is almost empty, but they have a wealth of love.

The Weasleys are fictional characters from a fantasy series, yet they live out the truths of the Gospel to a surprising degree. While their merits include sacrificing their safety in order to fight evil and injustice, their virtues are even evident in the more mundane daily practices in their home. In addition to the fierce and devoted love Arthur and Molly Weasley offer each other and their children, their home is a haven for the marginalized. Forgotten people who have nowhere else to go find a place at their kitchen table. It's easy to imagine Molly Weasley adding a little water to the soup after welcoming an unexpected guest, trusting that there will always be enough. Their home is a beautiful image of what Christian hospitality should be.

The reader sees this home through the eyes of Harry, orphaned as an infant with a small fortune inherited from his parents, who thinks the Burrow is the most wonderful place on earth. There he is welcomed with hot onion soup and people who care for him, protect his welfare, and seek his good. He gratefully dives into this chaotic space filled with love. The Burrow is contrasted with the sterile and exclusive Malfoy Manor—grand and gated but empty and joyless. It doesn't matter how much material wealth the Malfoys have . . . no one would want to be born into *their* family.

From the outside looking in, it's easy to see how lucky the Weasley children are to grow up in a joyful home with devoted parents and everything in the world that they truly need. But this isn't always evident to the kids. That's the heartbreaking truth that every parent has to deal with when raising children against the flow of consumerist culture. Even if a family becomes a school of love, a haven of hospitality, and a place of beautiful Christian sacrifice, there will still be struggles, and the goodness of what you seek to create may not be appreciated by your children, at least not until they are much older.

It's painful to watch young Ron Weasley's resentment over not having new school clothes or a fancy house; we know he's missing the fact that he is rich in more important ways. Harry would give anything to switch places with him. But like foolish Ron, our kids will always want more, just as we adults are prone to do. If we're not careful, the seeds of that same discontentment can grow in our own souls.

There are certainly moments when I start to compare our small, century-old starter home with a friend's big, beautiful house, thinking of how it would feel to have so much space and not be living on top of one another. It's easy to envy families that seem to have more when I lose sight of the fact that we've chosen to be Weasleys, not Malfoys, and that means simplicity, generosity, family-focused living, and doing work that we love—even if it's not very lucrative. Surely Molly Weasley herself had moments when she looked around her full-to-bursting-with-kids home and at her secondhand clothes and felt a twinge of discontentment. Sometimes guiding our children on this journey of finding joy in simplicity helps us remember why we're living this way in the first place.

GUIDING CHILDREN TO EMBRACE THE GRACE

My oldest son is the most generous soul I've ever known. Someone gives him candy? He can't wait to share with the rest of the family. He's outgrown a toy? He can't wait to find a younger child who will enjoy it. He loves giving gifts, making food, and expressing this beautiful generosity. I can't take credit for it because he came out of the womb with this generous spirit. Yet he's not untouched by the consumerist mind-set.

"When I grow up, I want to be rich and buy all the LEGO sets ever made!"

So how did we respond to his childish dream? Did we throw up our hands and give up on this whole against-the-grain experiment? Not at all. It was simply time for another of those formative conversations that our children will be able to draw from as they grow.

I asked my son recently if LEGOs really changed his life. "Do you feel like your life is different a week or two after you get a new LEGO set?"

"Well, it makes me happy to get one, and I like putting them together."

"But when you wake up in the morning after you're done, is life different? Are you a happier person?" I asked him.

"Well . . . no. I guess not. I don't feel any different at all."

At the time, I wasn't sure if the conversation would stick, but it did. He's mentioned to me several times that maybe it's not buying things that makes our lives better, that fills those gaps in our souls. Has he stopped wanting new LEGO sets? No, but a seed has been planted. In time that seed will grow, just as he does.

Our children being susceptible to brilliant marketing strategies shouldn't discourage us. I've seen *Mad Men*; I know how the advertising world works. Marketers are paid to convince us that we can't be happy without purchasing something. Even though we know the drill, it still works on us—and we're the grown-ups! If it works on adults, our kids are even more vulnerable to that kind of manipulation.

The American Psychological Association estimates that "advertisers spend more than 12 billion dollars per year to reach the youth market and that children view more than 40,000 commercials each year."[1]

Twelve billion dollars is a lot of money. It's money advertisers wouldn't spend if their techniques weren't incredibly successful. So we shouldn't beat ourselves up about the fact that the marketing is working on our kids, but we must commit ourselves to opening up these hard conversations with our children.

Finding the Grace of Enough:
Tips to Living the Gospel as a Family

The *Catechism* reminds us that "a wholesome family life can foster interior dispositions that are a genuine preparation for a living faith and remain a support for it throughout one's life" (*CCC*, 2225). What are practical things we can do to help our children not get caught up in the throwaway culture?

Model something better. This is the number one thing we can do. It starts with us. The most powerful things we can do to help our kids fight consumerism are to put people before things, pursue simplicity, and live generously.

Minimize the effects of advertising. This is another simple but crucial strategy if we wish to remove some of the influence of consumerism. As much as I admire my friends with screen-free homes, I'll admit right now that screen-free does not describe our family. We have Netflix for entertainment, and we use our laptops frequently. Almost every day our kids will stream something to watch, and as a blogger and writer I can often be found behind my computer. But we decided to draw the line at commercials. There are no commercials in our home.

This embargo extends to print media too. Several years ago I removed myself from the lists of the catalogs that would arrive in the mail because seeing the new season collection from Anthropologie was too much for me. (Once the catalog arrived in my mailbox, I was sure I could never be truly happy without those cute shoes and quirky skirts.)

Watch for teachable moments. We recently stayed in a hotel on a trip to visit family. We flipped on the TV to watch a movie and a commercial for "Snuggles My Dream Puppy" came on. It was a stuffed animal that made sounds if you patted its tummy and closed its eyes if you hugged it. If you left him alone, darling Snuggles would start to snore. This short commercial caused our five-year-old daughter to have an epiphany: to be happy she *must* have Snuggles My Dream Puppy.

I reminded her that when we arrived back home we were getting a goldendoodle, a real live dog, the kind that barks, licks, wags its tail, drools, eats, and poops. She could pat his tummy, hug him, and he would even snore if she left him alone. He would do much more than a stuffed animal because he was an actual dog. But no, that would not do.

"I don't care about a real dog! I want Snuggles My Dream Puppy!" she wailed. This commercial had convinced her that this stuffed animal would be better than a living, breathing dog. Of course, you can imagine the end of this story: The real dog, a two-year-old goldendoodle named Olaf, was a huge hit and brings a lot of joy to our family. Snuggles My Dream Puppy went on my daughter's Christmas list for Grandma and Grandpa, was adored for forty-eight hours, and was then completely forgotten and left to collect dust in the closet. She had been sure that not having Snuggles was the one thing keeping her from blissful happiness. There was no convincing her otherwise. Marketing is powerful. The best thing we can do to keep our kids from its influence is simply to remove the siren song of those commercials from their lives.

Do what you can, beginning today. What if your kids have been exposed to a steady stream of commercials for several years? Are they destined to be little consumerist robots? Not at all. You can always begin again to rewire those little minds, but like all worthwhile pursuits, it takes hard work and intentionality. Begin with decreasing your children's exposure to commercials as much as you can. Switch out cable for streaming services such as Netflix and Amazon Prime that give you more control as a parent over what is being viewed (and are significantly cheaper than cable).

Teach your children to think critically. It's important to help your children interpret what they're seeing when they inevitably come into contact with advertising. Children younger than four or five do not understand that what they're viewing is an advertisement rather than entertainment, and children younger than seven or eight do not understand that the intent of the marketing campaign is to persuade them.[2] Their stage of development makes them highly impressionable. They need help to discern what they're seeing and/or hearing.

When our oldest child started reading, he was suddenly able to read billboards all over town. "Mom! Shoe Station is having the *best sale of the year*! How exciting! Can we go?" It was like having a tiny Buddy the Elf in the back seat, ready to congratulate the makers of the world's best cup of coffee. We had to explain that what he was seeing was an advertisement created with the intent to persuade us to spend money on a company's product. Now as an older child, this is a concept he understands very well, but for younger children, this is very difficult to comprehend. It's up to us to identify advertising for our children, remind them that what they're seeing or hearing is shown to convince us to spend money and is presented by a biased party.

"But, Mom, the sign says it's a great deal."

"Yes, the company selling that product wants us to think so. But that isn't something we need, so it is not a good deal for our family."

Be smart shoppers. One facet of decreasing exposure to advertising in our daily lives is that we rarely take our kids into stores. This is partly to keep our own sanity because shopping with young children is like an Olympic sport. Instead of javelin or hammer throw, it's "keeping all small children from falling out of carts and grabbing items from shelves without yelling at them." Even the grocery store is designed to highlight products that kids want by putting them at child height, expecting that when our kids beg for them we will give in because it's easier than causing a scene in public.

Our grocery store has a blessed thing called curbside service, which means I can avoid the inevitable request for junk foods I wasn't planning to buy and I don't have to wrangle three kids through the store. For other things, if borrowing or secondhand fails, we stick with a list of what we actually need rather than browsing the enticing aisles.

This reinforces for our kids that buying things is not entertainment but rather a necessity of life.

Let your children participate in your charitable giving. Just as important as modeling good spending habits is modeling an alternative to consumerism. Involve your children in almsgiving in a way that will really engage them. Consider sponsoring a child or elderly person in need through a charity organization such as Unbound. You can even choose a sponsored friend your child's age, put their photo on the fridge, and help your child write letters to them. Connecting a face with the act of giving is so helpful to children. "No, we're not going out to eat because we're using that money to send to our sponsored friend's family so he has food and can go to school." This makes the need less ambiguous and really helps children participate with a cheerful heart.

Other families have the tradition of making "blessing bags" full of necessities such as water, snacks, toiletries, bus passes, and feminine hygiene products to keep in their car and pass to anyone in need that they encounter. Especially during liturgical seasons that focus on almsgiving, a family might involve their children in sacrificing by giving up eating meat once or twice a week to save that money for a charity chosen by the whole family. By opting to give rather than buy, we can help our children appreciate people over possessions.

But the heart of the matter is that our children will watch us. The most powerful antidote to the throwaway culture is when we model simplicity, hospitality, and generosity in the "the domestic church." In this school of love, the home, we aim to educate children in faith and charity so that they will not be taken in by the false promises of consumerism. In the midst of the throwaway culture, we must offer something better than the lies that surround them if our children are to follow us. Instead of an obsession with "more," we must model Christlike love for other people and God's creation so we can give our children gifts that endure.

I'm trying to find joy in the eternal so that my children can too. My prayer is that someday my children will see something beautiful in our crazy experiment and the goodness of what we wanted to offer them. In the meantime, I'll keep adding water to the soup and finding inspiration in my favorite magical family.

12

CHOOSING HOPE IN A DARK WORLD

Hope speaks to us of a thirst, an aspiration, a longing for a life of fulfillment, a desire to achieve great
things, things which fill our heart and lift our spirit to
lofty realities like truth, goodness and beauty, justice
and love.

—Pope Francis

My shirt stuck to my back in the sweltering July heat in
Milledgeville, Georgia. My friend Christy and I were walking up the steps to the front porch of the farmhouse that
was once home to famed twentieth-century Southern writer
Flannery O'Connor. A lone peacock sat mournfully in the
coop outside—a shadow of Flannery's beloved flock.

We were on a pilgrimage of sorts, making a visit to the
farmhouse where this unusual Catholic writer spent her
final years before she died of lupus in 1964. The crutches
she had to use during her later years were still by her bed,
as was her missal. In one corner was her typewriter and
the curtains she made herself from peacock feather–print
fabric; in another, a little picture of St. Thérèse of Lisieux
beside a doorframe. I took a deep breath, trying to wrap

my mind around the fact that I was in the home of one of my favorite writers.

It sounds strange that the woman who wrote short stories and novels in the Southern gothic style about serial killers, men who blind themselves, and boys who drown other children could be a conduit of grace to Daniel and me. But her writing was so influential on Daniel in particular that he doesn't know if he would even be Catholic today if he hadn't encountered her work. Flannery's stories led us deeper into a tale even more surprising than anything she penned: the Story with a capital S; the Story in which God loved us so much that he asked a human woman to be his mother, was born as a helpless infant, and came not just to live among us but to be murdered in an agonizing way—to conquer death once and for all.

Flannery's faith was always a matter of life and death to her. She's famous for responding to a claim that the Eucharist was merely symbolic with, "Well, if it's a symbol, to hell with it!"[1] It's either the precious Body and Blood of our Lord or who really cares?

The characters in her stories often come to understand that Christianity either matters not at all or it is everything and should completely transform us. As we were carried through our own story by God's grace, we began to agree with her. We were just two millennial kids who fell in love, got married, started a family, and entered the Church. But we realized that if we really accepted and lived out everything the Church taught, our lives would be strange, even alarming to the culture around us.

I've discovered that my penchant for changing my hair color and the sizable tattoo of Stella Maris, Our Lady Star of the Sea, on my right arm aren't what make me weird. Nobody really cares if I dye my hair pink. But when you give up most of your worldly goods and move to a farm with no toilets, don't use birth control, believe our extra resources actually belong to the poor, and would really like everyone to come over for dinner (and it's gonna take five hours), then you'll get some looks.

It won't stop there. No matter how inclusive and non-judgmental you are, some people are going to hate you. It's true. Merely trying to orient *your* life to the Gospel will call into question what the throwaway culture has been selling. This is why even St. Teresa of Calcutta, whose Missionaries of Charity serve the poorest of the poor and commit to seeing dignity in every human being, is often subjected to scorn and vitriol from the secular world.

The throwaway culture hates the Gospel and those who embrace it because Christianity is diametrically opposed to the consumerist culture of death. This culture cannot thrive where the culture of life is joyfully lived out. Wondering at the beauty in the world, rejecting consumerism, committing to home and family, sitting around the table together, opening your home, building your communities, loving generously—these things are a powerful threat to the throwaway culture and will be met with derision or cynicism at best.

But enough people are dissatisfied with what has been offered to them that if you choose something different than what the throwaway culture is selling, you'll have plenty of people say, "Tell me more." You'll have some people who want to come over for dinner—even if it takes five hours, *because* it will take five hours.

You'll have people who'll say, "So I'm not religious, but I'm really intrigued by this NFP thing. Can you give me more information?"

You'll have people tell you, "I want to live with less so that we can have more time together as a family."

That's where there's a strong foundation for hope. We are weary of the lies of throwaway culture. We know something has gone horribly wrong. When we reflect on the dire situation of our extreme consumerism—the damage done to God's earth, the isolation of human beings from one another and from God—it would be easy to despair or to run for the hills to seek shelter and escape. After all, what impact can we make? Can we really turn the tide of destruction, consumerism, selfish individualism, waste, familial break-down, disconnection from nature, and struggling communities? It seems a fool's errand. Should we just build an ark—maybe let in a chosen few and emerge when things look better and the storm has passed?

No, that's not really an option. Pope Francis reminds us that "encountering God does not mean fleeing from this world or turning our back on nature" (*LS* 235). We are called to *participate* in God's work of redemption for the world while living in the world. Sure, we'll always be the odd ones out, but is it possible to be a light to the world even when things look this dark? Yes. As St. John Paul II encourages us, "Do not abandon yourselves to despair. We are the Easter people and hallelujah is our song."[2]

To disregard the possibility of redemption would be to dismiss the way Christianity has always worked. Our faith is a religion featuring the impossible coming to fruition. To lose hope would be to forget what story is being lived out. We are a part of the cosmic story of God's love that surpasses any obstacle. Christians have always been told that our quest is foolish. Yet the gates of hell cannot prevail against the Church instituted by Christ himself. He is already victorious.

This truth glimmers even in our popular stories and fairy tales. Frodo could never destroy the ring. Narnians can never defeat the White Witch. Teenage wizards could never save the world from the most powerful dark sorcerer. An evil fairy's spell cannot be conquered by true love. Impossible! Yet a hobbit saves Middle-earth. The White Witch is defeated. Voldemort's regime falls. Sleeping Beauty wakes up. A foolish hope is grounded in the strength of love and prevails against seemingly insurmountable opposition. We tell these stories because we know deep in our hearts that they are telling us the truth.

We can fall prey to despair. We easily forget that the night is darkest before the dawn and the Gospel reveals the unexpected redemption—even when all hope seems lost. God himself becomes a defenseless infant in order to take on our humanity and save us. The surprising truth of hope prevails when a poor Jewish girl in the middle of nowhere becomes the Mother of God with the strength to crush Satan under her heel. Sacrificial love wins against the hold of sin on the world. When the disciples feared their faith in Jesus was for naught, we see love overcoming even sin and death in his Resurrection. An uneducated fisherman who betrays our Lord out of cowardice becomes the first pope and the rock upon which Christ builds his Church. This pattern of seemingly impossible events should give us hope that God can transform *us* and use us in his redemption of the world he created and loves.

Pope Francis reminds us: "How wonderful is the certainty that each human life is not adrift in the midst of hopeless chaos, in a world ruled by pure chance or endlessly recurring cycles! The Creator can say to each one of us: 'Before I formed you in the womb, I knew you' (Jer 1:5). We were conceived in the heart of God, and for this reason 'each of us is the result of a thought of God. Each of us is willed, each of us is loved, each of us is necessary'" (*LS* 65). We are not alone. We are not insignificant. We are part of the tapestry that is God's grand plan. We have a living hope in the person of Jesus Christ.

Our Christian faith holds hope as one of the three highest virtues. Our belief that we are called to play an integral part in God's redemption of his world is key. We are not without hope that we can successfully reject the throwaway culture and that the beauty of the Gospel can win the day. But to participate will require so much of us. Servant of God Dorothy Day notes that the "greatest challenge of the day is: how to bring about a revolution of the heart, a revolution which has to start with each one of us?"[3] We aren't given a checklist to mark off. We are asked to change our hearts, to allow God to transform them. That won't happen in a weekend. It can be discouraging to consider how far I am from what I know God has called me to be. But we have the saints to show us that this revolution of the heart is possible (and they cheer us on from heaven).

The longing for something beyond the throwaway culture becomes stronger and stronger as we yearn for what the culture of consumerism can never offer us. Things can only swing so far until they snap. Even secular movements that critique the throwaway culture and promote minimalism, simplicity, and community as an alternative are gaining momentum daily. While these movements don't show us the whole picture of the Gospel, they reveal the emptiness of our consumerism. We have experienced comfort beyond anything known in human history and we've still found life wanting because we were made for so much more: beauty, real relationships, traditions seeped in time, and even a willingness to sacrifice in order to choose "the greater part."

When I look around to those in my Catholic community, both online and local, I see great commitment to living out the Gospel. I think this is partly due to the swinging back I mentioned, but also because in a world so permeated with the throwaway culture, if you're not going to live out your faith, why keep showing up? Going against the grain to follow Christ's call isn't easy. If you're not serious about it, you just wouldn't identify with faith anymore. Perhaps this is just anecdotal, but it seems to be supported by some noticeable trends. The shift in the millennial generation can be demonstrated by such symptoms as great numbers of millennials discerning calls to the priesthood and religious life as opposed to the post–Vatican II generation (those born from 1961 to 1981) during which there was a decrease in vocations and interest in the priesthood or religious life.[4]

This is not to say that only millennial Catholics are committed to living out the Gospel, that all millennial Catholics are devout, or that there is no "revolution of the heart" in baby boomer and post–Vatican II Catholics. By no means. But it does mean that something exciting is happening. In a world that is more and more incompatible with Christian thought, perhaps we are taking our faith *more* seriously, not less. There is reason for hope.

In the words of Flannery, "You shall know the truth and the truth shall make you odd."[5] The truth sets us free, but it also transforms us. If we cling to the Cross, we will never be accepted by the throwaway culture. But we have something better to offer, something based in a living hope. As much as the throwaway culture seeks to distort our view, its inability to satisfy in any real way offers a great opportunity to share the Gospel by our lives. If your life looks completely insane to the throwaway culture, it will also be attractive to those who are seeking an alternative. This is why Christianity *should* seem not just absurd but irrelevant to a culture of consumerism. It doesn't fit in that schema; it cannot.

According to Pope Francis, hope "involves taking risks. It means being ready not to be seduced by what is fleeting, by false promises of happiness, by immediate and selfish pleasures, by a life of mediocrity and self-centeredness, which only fills the heart with sadness and bitterness. No, hope is bold; it can look beyond personal convenience, the petty securities and compensations which limit our horizon, and can open us up to grand ideals which make life more beautiful and worthwhile."[6]

This is my prayer for myself and for you. My failures are often a failure of hope. I am easily seduced by the fleeting, the false, the selfish. I often settle for mediocrity and self-centeredness. But I know you and I both want *more*. G. K. Chesterton notes that the "Christian ideal has not been tried and found wanting. It has been found difficult; and left untried."[7] Let's be bold with our hope. Let's pray for the strength to look beyond convenience and the false promise of security the throwaway culture offers us. May we have eyes to see beyond those lies and dive deep into Christian life. May we understand the world around us through the lens of the Gospel and seek to live it out.

Finding the Grace of Enough: Tips for Living with Hope

Choosing hope can seem like an abstract goal. How do we choose hope in practical ways?

Form a moral imagination. Encounter the lives of the saints and holy men and women in spiritual reading. Immerse yourself in stories (even fictional tales) that offer the truth of hope overcoming darkness.

Practice prayer and seek spiritual guidance during times when you are tempted to despair (or seek professional help if you're experiencing a season of prolonged depression). Most of us will fight this battle of hope in very small ways, but don't make the mistake of diminishing the value of those seemingly small things.

Remember that, in the words of Dante, it's love that "moves the sun and the other stars." Just as the deep magic of Narnia was incomprehensible to the White Witch, weapons we can wield against consumerism are weapons the throwaway culture does not understand or value: beauty, home, generosity, hospitality, community, wonder. But love is the truly powerful force that our hope for a better world is anchored in. The truth may make us odd, but it will also make us capable of living against the grain of a culture that does not understand the Gospel. We can begin by inviting our neighbors over for dinner, because that's the sort of thing that changes the world.

CONCLUSION:
BEYOND THE SHIRE

Our adventure of moving to the farm, saying "enough!" to the throwaway culture, and starting a new kind of life may have officially begun in 2015 when we left our life in Florida for a year of milking goats and living in community—without so much as a flushing toilet. But it didn't end there.

It would be easy to look at our experience on the farm as some kind of bucolic ideal: our children running around in the sunshine and flowers, growing our own food and sharing meals in the beautiful countryside, roosters crowing in the distance, snuggling baby animals all day. It certainly didn't always feel idyllic—it was exhausting, muddy, sweaty, and challenging in many ways, granted—but it was a year we will treasure forever.

Does shifting away from the toxic throwaway culture have to be a pastoral experience? Does it require an impossible nostalgic re-creation of Tolkien's Hobbiton, of little isolated rural communities where everyone is a farmer?

Rural life has a beauty and goodness all its own. But moving our entire population to rural farms is neither possible nor what the opposition to the throwaway culture is all about. Besides, spending too much time daydreaming about a countryside utopia can cause an otherwise positive cultural vision to be written off as wishful thinking. Instead, what if we sought something greater, something possible from wherever God has placed us: an apartment in Boston, Massachusetts, a duplex in Charlotte, North Carolina, or a starter home in Waco, Texas? The goodness of our experience at the farm and what makes the Shire truly noteworthy isn't peculiar to country living. Among the treasures of hobbit culture are a relationship-centered community, a strong connection to the natural world, and the prioritization of leisure and festivity over production and efficiency. These things are completely opposed to our throwaway culture and compatible with the Gospel, and they can be lived out wherever you are. Perhaps what we need isn't to all retreat to little homogenous communities in the country where we feel comfortable. Perhaps what will truly be redemptive is to embrace the truths of the Gospel so completely that the revolutionary way we order our lives impacts the communities where we live and wherever we are becomes a little bit more like the Shire.

It's easy to get wrapped up in examining what grand global changes and political systems are most conducive to living out our Christian faith. These are worthy questions and discussions. But what we mustn't forget is that we can start a life of pursuing less and living more ordered toward the Gospel *right now*, in our homes, in our relationships, in our communities. Today we can invite someone over to dinner, read an extra bedtime story to our kids, fill our spaces with music and art that lift our hearts to God, and embrace other small but valuable practices that will change the world. Perhaps these changes must ripple out from our dining room tables, through our families, to our neighbors, into our communities.

When we decided to pursue the internship at the farm, our expectation was that afterward we would become full-time farmers with a big piece of land out in the country. Yet here we are two years later in a tiny house in the city. We'd still love to have our own piece of land someday, but what we discovered from our adventure is that the kind of life we wanted doesn't have to be lived on a farm.

As I write, it's Epiphany of 2018. While we don't live at the farm anymore, in some ways we've brought the farm to us with rows of vegetables growing and chickens squawking in our yard. Daniel has beehives all over town, and he's got big plans for goats to join the hens in our backyard. We built our own greenhouse and will plant fruit trees soon. The city would probably prefer that our cow, Taco, continue grazing at the farm rather than in the neighborhood, but he's very well behaved and comes when you call his name, so maybe we can work something out. We are close enough to walk to our parish (where our homeschool co-op also meets) so that we can be involved in our local Catholic community. We are certainly urban these days, but we are hardly isolated. We have great neighbors and a city we love.

Daniel just accepted a new job at a wonderful nonprofit where he'll be working with at-risk youth. The campus is so close to our hundred-year-old house that he can walk there, so we don't have to get a second vehicle. And his new schedule will mean more family time, something we've discovered is incredibly important to our home life.

While this book project is coming to a close, our family is beginning a new adventure. With my computer on my lap, I have a great view of my swelling belly reminding me that in just a few months our family will be blessed by a new life, a soul of infinite worth.

We are certainly not hobbits merrily frolicking in the green hills of the Shire all day. While we may have more livestock in our backyard than we used to, from the outside our lives look very similar to our lives in Florida: homeowners in the city, wrangling life with lots of small children. But the truth is, we've been deeply changed by our crazy experiment. The experience of dropping everything to pursue less and live more revealed the important things. We bonded as a family in a new way. We defined the good things that we would seek together: beauty, a home-centered life, hospitality, simplicity, honoring God by caring for his earth, community, hope. We're right smack-dab in the midst of life. We're trying to keep up with the laundry and driving to jiujitsu lessons. We're making dinner with friends and staying up too late talking around the table. Our lives may not be lived in Hobbiton, but I love what we're building together. It is enough. It is more than enough.

Acknowledgments

Without the enthusiastic support of my husband, Daniel, and our three oldest kids—Benjamin, Lucy, and Gwen—this book could never have materialized. Not just this book but the adventures described in it are all thanks to your presence in my life, sweet family. Thanks are also due to the two people who took the greatest pains to teach me to write: my loving mother, Margot Payne, and my college professor and friend Dr. Ralph C. Wood.

I am forever indebted to Heidi Hess Saxton for believing in this project, her editing brilliance, and her incomparable kindness. To all my longsuffering friends who read over chapters or gave feedback—including Cari Donaldson, Abbey Dupuy, Bonnie Engstrom, Laura Fanucci, Boze Herrington, Christy Isinger, Reid Makowsky, Kelly Mantoan, Luke Mitchell, Nell O'Leary, Sarah Ortiz, Mandi Richards, Kendra Tierney, and Molly Walter—I owe you all dinner and undying loyalty.

Brandon Vogt, your foreword was everything I dreamed it would be and more. I'm so grateful. I am also in the debt of other creatives, including Tsh Oxenreider, Jennifer Fulwiler, and Hallie Lord, who have blazed the trail and generously shared their wisdom with me.

This project would not have been possible without the great team at Ave Maria Press, my kind and supportive blog readers and podcast listeners, and my wonderful friends and family members who make life so beautiful.

REFLECTION QUESTIONS

These questions can be explored on your own or in a group discussion.

1. No Turning Back: Trading Security for Togetherness

1. It can be easy to get stuck in the conventional pursuit of affluence that is neither satisfying nor, for many in our post-recession society, even possible. What are some ways you could make do with less and spend more time with those you love?
2. Life on a sustainable farm isn't for everyone. What is your "dream" job? What are some of the quality-of-life issues that are most important to you?
3. What are small but significant changes you can make to live out countercultural Gospel virtues in your own life?

2. Simplicity, the Path to Authentic Freedom

1. What is the relationship between simplicity, the Christian virtue of *detachment* (see CCC, 2548, 2556), and Christ's commandment to "love your neighbor as yourself" (Mk 12:31)?
2. How might you go about determining if you have more possessions than you need? How might your possessions be overwhelming you, distracting you, and eating up your valuable time? Can you think of a recent example when your possessions got in the way of your relationships with those you love?
3. How can you pare down what you own and have a healthier attitude toward possessions? How can you offer your excess to those who don't have enough?

3. Nurturing a Wondrous Love for the Land

1. The *Catechism* teaches us to have respect for the integrity of creation (see CCC, 2415–2418). "Animals, like plants and inanimate beings, are by nature destined for the common good of past, present, and future humanity" (CCC, 2415; see also Gn 1:28–31). What are some ways you and your family can show respect for creation?

155

2. Haley and her family experienced a newfound sense of appreciation for creation on the farm, yet she acknowledges that not everyone is called to live a rural life. What practical steps can *you* take to regularly find awe and beauty in God's creation?
3. As you read this chapter, how were you challenged to rethink certain habits or practices of yours that might lead to waste or damage to the earth? What small changes can you make in how you eat that will support practices that honor God's creatures and his world?

4. Rediscovering Beauty by Attending to the Transcendent

1. The *Catechism's* teachings on truth, beauty, and sacred art are found under the eighth commandment: "You shall love your neighbor as yourself." Why do you suppose rediscovering beauty is an important antidote to commercialism and throwaway culture?
2. If "art is not an absolute end in itself, but is ordered to and ennobled by the ultimate end of man" (CCC, 2501), we honor God when we give and receive what is true, good, and beautiful. How often do you make space in your day for beauty? How might you do this more often?
3. In your daily home life, how can you incorporate times of quiet, lovely music, and other beautiful art that can help you lift your heart to God? How can you make your home a more beautiful space?

5. Making Home a Priority, a School of Love

1. Have you "wasted time" with your family today? In what ways do you treat your home like a hotel and your real life as what happens at work? In what ways can you seek to prioritize your home and family?
2. How often do you eat meals as a family (or, if you are single, seek out opportunities to share a meal in community)? It may not be possible for you to sit down together three times each day, but how might it be possible to eat more meals together?
3. What simple prayers, devotions, or other family traditions can you cultivate to nurture your family or community life?

6. The Five-Hour Dinner: Redeeming the Table with Slow Food

1. While fishing and hunting can be enjoyable pastimes for some, some people might have difficulty teaching their young children the "hard facts of life" in this way. What did you think of this part of Haley's story? What is the connection between buying locally grown meat and produce and being good stewards of the earth?

2. What are some of the characteristics of "slow food" that distinguish it from the kind of hospitality that is an expression of throwaway culture? Think of the preparations, the guest list, the meal itself, and how the guests interact with one another. How do these two kinds of events compare? Which is more attractive?

3. While this particular model of "slow food" offers a unique expression of hospitality, it isn't always a practical model for those who are stretched just to make time for an impromptu potluck gathering. What are the essential elements of Christian hospitality that you discovered in this chapter that could be incorporated into your everyday life?

7. Holy Hospitality: Welcoming Christ in the Stranger

1. In this chapter Haley speaks of the Eucharist as "the ultimate hospitality," when God draws us to his own table to give us not just the "fruit of the vine" but his own divine life. How do the origins of this sacrament (see Lk 22:7–20) speak to the importance of personal connection through the gift of hospitality?

2. Have you ever known a "Kevin," someone who drifts into your life in a casual way, clearly outside your regular social circle but just as clearly in need of a friend? What part of this story resonates with you the most? What do you think are prudent guidelines for stretching outside your comfort zone while protecting those entrusted to your care?

3. This particular chapter focuses on how we welcome the stranger in the name of Christ. Who are the coworkers, fellow parishioners, or neighbors who look like they might need the comfort of a meal and the company you can provide? How can you make hospitality a consistent part of your life, a practice that fits your unique gifts and situation?

8. Rebuilding Our Broken Communities

1. Jesus teaches that the second greatest commandment is to "love your neighbor as yourself" (Jn 13:34; see also *CCC*, 2196). Haley

starts out this chapter by describing her community in Waco, Texas—warts and all. How would you describe your neighborhood, your community? Do you know it well enough to be able to describe it as intimately as she did? If not, how might you change that?

2. How do you serve your community? What are some of the gifts you possess that could enrich your community and help meet the needs of your neighbors?

3. "The Church is not a little tribe of people like me. . . . It's filled with people with whom I have nothing in common. . . . We are not comfortable together. But we are one" (p. 101). How does this compare with your experience of parish life? What is the value of investing time and effort in those outside your "tribe"?

9. The Internet: Isolator or Community Builder?

1. In his 2004 message "The Media and the Family: A Risk and a Richness," Pope John Paul II spoke of social media's "exceptional opportunities for enriching the lives not only of individuals but also of families." Yet just a couple of paragraphs later, he acknowledges "the capacity to do grave harm . . . by presenting an inadequate or even deformed outlook on life, on the family, on religion, and on morality" (para. 2). How have you seen this played out in your life?

2. How has technology been a positive connector in your life? What are some examples of healthy ways that we can nurture relationships online? At what point does technology cease to be a tool and becomes a trap?

3. Haley identified two cultural trends that drove the need for "virtual connection" through the internet as a substitute for authentic connection and knowledge—what Pope Francis calls the "false sense of knowing." How might this be true in your own life? How do you set healthy boundaries so that technology does not become an unhealthy distraction from authentic relationships or from better understanding the world—and teach your family to cultivate these boundaries for themselves?

10. Generous Love: Discovering Authentic Intimacy

1. Haley calls their decision to stop using contraception "the adventure of a lifetime." How does this description resonate with you? What do you think is the best and most persuasive argument for using natural family planning?

2. Is being open to life an idea that is overwhelming or scary to you? How can you prepare your heart to seek generous love through spiritual growth and discipleship?

3. If you are married, how might you and your spouse talk about the theology of the body? If you are unmarried, how can you as a single person offer generous love to others?

11. Living the Gospel, Molly Weasley–Style

1. One of the most important ways we can model generous Gospel living is by being generous with God. For parents, this includes trusting God if he should call one or more of their children to serve him in a call to religious life. "Parents should welcome and respect with joy and thanksgiving the Lord's call to one of their children . . . in the consecrated life or in priestly ministry" (CCC, 2233). How might you react if one or more of your children were called to religious life?

2. What conversations and practices can you incorporate into your family life that will help your children participate in Gospel living? In ways big and small, how are you teaching them by example to show their love for God with their gifts and offerings, and to respond generously and prudently to the needs of others?

3. What consumerist influences can you remove from your home? What projects can you work on as a family that model generosity?

12. Choosing Hope in a Dark World

1. Think of a time when you felt despair over the state of the world. How did you find (or at what point did you decide to start finding) your way back to hope? Who are some of your favorite examples of people who choose to dwell in hope?

2. Haley recounts a number of literary examples of characters in fiction who muddled their way through, despite the darkness, to hope. How do these stories resonate with your experience? How can you choose hope despite the darkness? How might prayer and spiritual reading edify you? What stories inspire you to be hopeful even during difficult times?

3. What are some of your favorite ways to instill hope in others? What is one thing you can do to break the hold of throwaway culture in your part of the world?

NOTES

Introduction: Throwaway Culture and Its Revolutionary Gospel Antidote

1. Flannery O'Connor, "This Day in Letters, 6 September (1955): Flannery O'Connor to Betty Hester," *The American Reader*, accessed October 9, 2017, http://theamericanreader.com/6-september-1955-flannery-oconnor.

2. Simplicity, the Path to Authentic Freedom

1. Jeanne E. Arnold, Anthony P. Graesch, Enzo Ragazzini, and Elinor Ochs, *Life at Home in the Twenty-First Century: 32 Families Open Their Doors* (Los Angeles: Cotsen Institute of Archaeology Press, 2012), 24.

2. Arnold et al., *Life at Home in the Twenty-First Century*, 36.

3. C. S. Lewis, *The Weight of Glory* (San Francisco: HarperOne, 2001), 26.

4. Basil the Great, *On Social Justice* (Crestwood, NY: St. Vladimir's Seminary Press, 2009), 69.

5. Benedict XVI, "Address of His Holiness Benedict XVI to the German Pilgrims Who Had Come to Rome for the Inauguration Ceremony of the Pontificate," Libreria Editrice Vaticana, April 25, 2005, https://w2.vatican.va/content/benedict-xvi/en/speeches/2005/april/documents/hf_ben-xvi_spe_20050425_german-pilgrims.html.

3. Nurturing a Wondrous Love for the Land

1. Arnold et al., *Life at Home in the Twenty-First Century*, 69.

2. Thomas Dubay, *The Evidential Power of Beauty: Science and Theology Meet* (San Francisco: Ignatius Press, 1999), 175.

3. Benedict XVI, "Letter to the Ecumenical Patriarch of Constantinople on the Occasion of the Seventh Symposium of the Religion, Science and the Environment Movement," Libreria Editrice Vaticana, September 1, 2007, http://w2.vatican.va/content/benedict-xvi/en/letters/2007/documents/hf_ben-xvi_let_20070901_symposium-environment.html.

4. G. K. Chesterton, *St. Thomas Aquinas: The Dumb Ox* (New York: Image, 1974), 11.

5. John Paul II, "Apostolic Journey to the United States of America and Canada, Mass for the Rural Workers," Libreria Editrice Vaticana, September 17, 1987, https://w2.vatican.va/content/john-paul-ii/en/homilies/1987/documents/hf_jp-ii_hom_19870917_messa-agricoltori.html.

6. G. K. Chesterton, *What's Wrong with the World?* (New York: Dover Publications, 2012), 69.

4. Rediscovering Beauty by Attending to the Transcendent

1. Augustine, *Sermons*, vol. 3, bk. 7, in *The Works of Saint Augustine: A Translation for the 21st Century* (New York: New City Press, 1994), 70.

2. Olivia Rudgard, "One in Six Young People Are Christian as Visits to Church Buildings Inspire Them to Convert," *Telegraph*, June 17, 2017, http://www.telegraph.co.uk/news/2017/06/17/one-six-young-people-christian-visits-church-buildings-inspire.

3. Robert Barron, "To Evangelize Through Beauty," *Catholic News Agency*, February 19, 2013, http://www.catholicnewsagency.com/column/to-evangelize-through-beauty-2476.

4. Benedict XVI, "Homily on Dedication of the Church of the Holy Family in Spain," *Catholic Online*, November 8, 2011, http://www.catholic.org/news/international/europe/story.php?id=39065.

5. Fyodor Dostoevsky, *The Idiot* (London: Penguin Classics, 2004), 446.

6. Chesterton, *What's Wrong with the World?*, 192.

7. MewithoutYou, "Messes of Men," track 1 on *Brother, Sister*, Tooth and Nail Records, 2006, audio CD.

8. Lewis, *The Weight of Glory*, 42.

5. Making Home a Priority, a School of Love

1. Wendell Berry, *The Art of the Commonplace: The Agrarian Essays of Wendell Berry* (Berkeley, CA: Counterpoint, 2005), 67.

2. "Pope Francis to Married Couples: You Must Waste Time with Your Children," Catholic Archdiocese of Sydney (website), October 28, 2013, https://www.sydneycatholic.org/news/latest_news/2013/20131028_1216.shtml.

3. Thérèse of Lisieux, *The Story of a Soul* (Washington, DC: ICS Publications, 1996), 242.

4. Berry, *The Art of the Commonplace*, 67.

5. Lucinda Secrest McDowell, *The Role of a Lifetime: Your Part in God's Story* (Nashville: B and H Books, 2008), 57.

6. The Five-Hour Dinner: Redeeming the Table with Slow Food

1. Berry, *The Art of the Commonplace*, 324.

7. Holy Hospitality: Welcoming Christ in the Stranger

1. Teresa of Calcutta, *Where There Is Love, There Is God: Her Path to Closer Union with God and Greater Love for Others* (New York: Image, 2012), 329.

2. Dorothy Day, "Aims and Purposes of the Catholic Worker Movement," *Catholic Worker*, February 1940, https://cjd.org/about/what-is-the-catholic-worker-movement.

8. Rebuilding Our Broken Communities

1. Sarah Pulliam Bailey, "Rob Bell, the Pastor Who Questioned Hell, Is Now Surfing, Working with Oprah, and Loving Life in L.A.," *Huffington Post*, December 2, 2014, http://www.huffingtonpost.com/2014/12/02/rob-bell-oprah_n_6256454.html.

2. Rumer Godden, *In This House of Brede* (New York: Loyola Classics, 2005), 26.

9. The Internet: Isolator or Community Builder?

1. C. S. Lewis, *The Four Loves* (San Francisco: HarperOne, 2017), 155.

10. Generous Love: Discovering Authentic Intimacy

1. John Paul II, *Love and Responsibility* (San Francisco: Ignatius Press, 1993), 42.

2. NFP is an umbrella term for several science-based methods of following a woman's natural rhythms of monthly fertility by monitoring her fertility symptoms such as waking (basal) temperature. NFP and FAM are not to be confused with the highly ineffective and archaic "rhythm method," and are proven to be effective not just in postponing pregnancy but also in achieving pregnancy and pinpointing possible women's health issues.

11. Living the Gospel, Molly Weasley–Style

1. "Report of the APA Task Force on Advertising and Children," *American Psychological Association*, accessed January 16, 2018. http:// www.apa.org/pubs/info/reports/advertising-children.aspx.

2. "Report of the APA Task Force on Advertising and Children," *American Psychological Association*, accessed January 16, 2018, http:// www.apa.org/pubs/info/reports/advertising-children.aspx.

12. Choosing Hope in a Dark World

1. Flannery O'Connor, *The Habit of Being: Letters of Flannery O'Connor* (New York: Farrar, Straus and Giroux, 1988), 125.

2. Peter Hebblethwaite, *Pope John Paul II and the Church* (Kansas City: Sheed and Ward, 1995), 68.

3. Dorothy Day, *Loaves and Fishes* (Maryknoll, NY: Orbis Books, 1997), 215.

4. Tim Drake, "CARA Study Finds Abundance of Potential Priests and Sisters," *National Catholic Register*, October 9, 2012, http://www.ncregister.com/daily-news/ cara-study-finds-abundance-of-potential-priests-and-sisters.

5. Ralph Wood, *Flannery O'Connor and the Christ-Haunted South* (Grand Rapids: Eerdmans, 2005), 160.

6. Francis, "Address of His Holiness Pope Francis to Students," Libreria Editrice Vaticana, September 20, 2015, https://w2.vatican. va/content/francesco/en/speeches/2015/september/documents/ papa-francesco_20150920_cuba-giovani.html.

7. Chesterton, *What's Wrong with the World?* 29.

Resources

Decluttering

Heasley, Ann Marie. "40 Bags in 40 Days Decluttering Challenge." *White House Black Shutters*. http://www.whitehouseblack shutters.com/40-bags-in-40-days. Accessed February 15, 2018.

Oxenreider, Tsh. *Organized Simplicity: The Clutter-Free Approach to Intentional Living*. Blue Ash, OH: Betterway Home, 2010.

Sperry, Mary. *Making Room for God: Decluttering and the Spiritual Life*. Notre Dame, IN: Ave Maria Press, 2018.

Natural Family Planning

Billings, Evelyn. *The Billings Method: Using the Body's Natural Signal of Fertility to Achieve or Avoid Pregnancy*. Herefordshire, UK: Gracewing, 2011.

FertilityCare Centers of America. FertilityCare.org (Creighton Model).

Fisher, Simcha. *The Sinner's Guide to Natural Family Planning*. Huntington, IN: Our Sunday Visitor, 2014.

Marquette University: Natural Family Planning. https://nfp.marquette.edu.

Weschler, Toni. *Taking Charge of Your Fertility: The Definitive Guide to Natural Birth Control, Pregnancy Achievement, and Reproductive Health*. New York: William Morrow, 2006.

West, Christopher. *Good News About Sex and Marriage: Answers to Your Honest Questions About Catholic Teaching*. Cincinnati, OH: Servant, 2004.

World Organisation of Ovulation Method Billings. http://woomb.org.

Prayer and Liturgical Year

Clayton, David, and Leila Marie Lawler. *The Little Oratory: A Beginner's Guide to Praying in the Home*. Bedford, NH: Sophia Institute Press, 2014.

Faehnle, Michele, and Emily Jaminet. *Divine Mercy for Moms: Sharing the Lessons of St. Faustina*. Notre Dame, IN: Ave Maria, 2016.

Gould, Meredith. *The Catholic Home: Celebrations and Traditions for Holidays, Feast Days, and Every Day.* New York: Image, 2006.

Hendey, Lisa M., and Sarah A. Reinhard, eds. *The Catholic Mom's Prayer Companion: A Book of Daily Reflections.* Notre Dame, IN: Ave Maria Press, 2016.

Smiley, Kendra. *Mother of the Year: 365 Days of Encouragement for Devoted Moms.* Savage, MN: Broadstreet, 2017.

Stewart, Daniel, and Haley Stewart. *Feast! Real Food, Reflections, and Simple Living for the Christian Year.* CreateSpace, 2013.

———. *More Feasts! Celebrating Saints and Seasons with Simple Real Food Recipes.* E-book, PDF, 2014.

Tierney, Kendra. *The Catholic All Year Compendium.* San Francisco: Ignatius Press, 2018.

Haley Stewart is a Catholic author, podcaster, and speaker who previously served as publications specialist and project coordinator at The Center for Christian Ethics at Baylor University. She also worked as a ballet instructor and rehearsal assistant at the South Georgia Ballet.

Stewart coauthored *Feast! Real Food, Reflections,* and *Simple Living for the Christian Year* with her husband, Daniel. She has contributed to *America* magazine, *Verily, Catholic Exchange, The Art of Simple,* and *Aleteia.* Stewart has appeared on CatholicTV, Relevant Radio, The Catholic Channel on SiriusXM Radio, Iowa Catholic Radio, and Real Life Radio.

She lives with her family in Waco, Texas.

Facebook: Carrots for Michaelmas
Podcast: fountainsofcarrots.com
Twitter: @HaleyCarrots
Instagram: HaleyCarrots
Pinterest: Haley of Carrots

Brandon Vogt is a bestselling and award-winning author, blogger, and speaker who serves as content director for Bishop Robert Barron's Word on Fire Catholic Ministries.